From One to
Ninety-one:
A Life

Maggie Thompson

Maggie

PUBLISHED BY
UNIVERSITY OF ORANGE
BRIDGEBUILDER PRESS

U of O
A Free University of the People

7/16/11

Printed by
Off the Common Books
Amherst, Massachusetts

ISBN 978-1-937146-02-3

DEDICATION

*To Mindy and Josh, and all the other
beautiful people I have loved*

ACKNOWLEDGMENTS

I feel like one of the luckiest people in the world when I realize how many friends and members of my family have helped me since I innocently said, "I think I'll write my memoirs."

First off is Serena Crystal who, with some help from Roy, edited the entire manuscript, remedying my dislike of commas. Pam Shaw designed a cover which I love and refused to bill me. Rich Brown put the text to print, not a small task considering how long I ran on. And Mindy and Lily did the heavy lifting of preparing all the pictures. Molly Kaufman, my granddaughter, and Herb Way, the photographer, helped along the way. I would also like to thank all of the people who cheered me on or jogged my memory. I couldn't have done it without you.

Cover art: painted by Samuel M. Koenigsberg, with whom I was working in 1956, to celebrate my birthday.

TABLE OF CONTENTS

Twenty years from now you will be more disappointed
by the things you didn't do than the ones you did do.
So throw off the bowlines. Sail away from the safe harbor.
Catch the tradewinds in your sails.
Explore. Dream. Discover.

—Mark Twain

I
CHILLICOTHE

My father, Don McKinley Brown, so named because he was born in 1896 while William McKinley was running for the U.S. presidency, was raised on a farm at Swanton, Ohio, near Toledo. His father, William Brown, was Pennsylvania Dutch, the name given to Germans who tarried there before moving on. His mother, Margaret Egnew, was a native of Ireland.

1.1 Don Brown

Don had barely finished high school when he was drafted into the army during World War I. He was sent to Chillicothe, Ohio, where he was in the Quartermaster Corps. At a dance one night he met and liked Minnie Hall, a proud native of Morgan County in southern Ohio. Her father, Jacob Hall, was of English extraction. Her mother, Margaret Barry, was the daughter of an English girl who had run away with an Irish sailor and come to America. Minnie had been brought up in the Liberty Hill Church where she acquired a strong sense of right and wrong that stayed with her all her life. She attended the Normal School at Ohio University in Athens and at the age of 16 became a teacher.

She had taught two years when she contracted tuberculosis and was sent to Asheville, North Carolina~famous as a healing climate~to recuperate. The Vanderbilts and the Morgans, united in marriage, had built a fabulous estate called Biltmore outside of Asheville. It included a hospital. When Minnie recovered her health, she entered its nurses' training program. It took three years and was rigorous and extremely professional. There was no tuition and the student nurses were paid $5 a month. The course completed, Minnie did some nursing at the hospital and on private duty. When the war broke out, food prices rose so that by 1917, for example, it cost $1 to buy one orange. Minnie headed home to Ohio and got a job at Chillicothe Hospital in time to help people stricken in the 1917-20 influenza pandemic that killed at least five million people worldwide, most of its victims being healthy young adults.

1.2 Minnie Brown

Imagine how she felt when she learned that Don, the nice young man she had met at a dance, had come down with the dreaded "Spanish Flu" and was among her patients. She nursed him back to health. They fell in love and were married in the Methodist Church in March of 1919.

It was a happy but brief honeymoon. I was born nine months later.

Whether I shall turn out to be the heroine of my own life these pages will show.[1]

---

1   A tip of the hat to Pip of *Great Expectations!*

II
CHIPPEWA
(1919-1933)

When my father and mother married, the doctors told her that if she did not get him to the country, he would not live. They sojourned for a while in Dayton, Ohio, where I was born, then moved north, settling in Chippewa Lake, a pin-point on the map 35 miles southwest of Cleveland. They rented a small house on the main street, truly the main street since it was the only one. Mom used to recount that there were holes in the floor and I delighted in poking things, including whatever of her jewelry I could find, down the holes to

2.1 Maggie at one

hear them splash into the water in the basement. Dad nicknamed Mom "Peggy," and the name stuck.

Dad got a job selling sugar wholesale. To get around, he bought a horse and buggy. To care for them, he rented a barn and put in a ton of hay. In quick succession the horse had a heart attack and died, the barn that stored the buggy and hay burned down, and there was a sudden and severe drop in the sugar market. Dad applied for and got a job with the U.S. Post Office as a rural mail carrier on a salary of $200 a month. He had to furnish his own transportation. Over the years it would include riding a horse when the roads were impassable.

My parents found a 20-acre farm about half a mile from town

selling for $2,000 and they bought it. It stretched for about a quarter of a mile along the country road and back to a small creek and a hill that extended the whole length of the property. There were a pretty maple tree and a large evergreen in the front yard. The east side had a wonderful sweet cherry tree, perfect for climbing in season. To the right was an apple orchard, with sour cherries along the side facing the house. Bordering the creek were large weeping willows. Mom named the place Willowdale. Both parents took great pride in making their home attractive. They built a white picket fence between the lawn and the two-acre field on the east and planted a lot of shrubbery, including a front hedge and a taller hedge to shield the barn from the house. They constructed a small fishpond in the backyard.

For many months Dad had his eye on a lovely white lilac on the grounds of a deserted house. One spring evening after dark, he bundled all of us into the car, drove us there and, while Mom held the flashlight, dug up that magnificent bush, big enough to be called a tree. Feeling exuberant, we took it home and he planted it in our backyard where it survived and thrived and, for all I know, may continue to this day. One other bush we cherished flowered with little yellow blossoms and a red center. It smelled like spice-cinnamon or cloves. We never knew its name but in later years always wished we could find it again.

A family of groundhogs inhabited the hill. In the long field on top, my father planted an orchard of apples alternated with peaches, the theory being that it took the apples a long time to mature, and the peach trees would, in the meantime, mature, bear fruit and die. By the time I was in college, they were in glorious harvest. I arrived home from a camp counselor's job in time to help sort and sell the peaches. They were luscious and I ate so many that for the first time in my life I broke out in hives. I was being driven to distraction when an old lady told me how to cure them. The secret is the application of one's own urine. It worked like a charm. One treatment did it.

The creek flowing through our land was situated at the foot of a high precipice, out of which flowed a spring producing pure cold water. My father brought electricity to the town for the first time (at a cost of $200, no small sum) after which anyone in Chippewa could hook on without charge. He harnessed the spring to supply all our needs both in the house and the barn. Goodbye to the outhouse, hello to a real bathroom carved out of one of the bedrooms.

Our creek played a major role in my young life. It became a favorite playground where I spent hours wading, in an always futile attempt to catch crayfish. The water was icy cold on my bare feet and large willow trees along the banks shaded me. No one I knew was ever intrigued to join me, but I found it heavenly and worked at it tirelessly. And in the fall there was an additional attraction. Beside the creek grew a large hickory nut tree. Every fall I spent hours trying to crack the nuts between stones. The result was nutmeats covered with sand but utterly heavenly. No one ever joined me, but I found the enterprise soul-satisfying.

One summer I built a miniature golf course alongside the creek, copying holes I had seen in real miniature courses. A few of them were quite creditable. We played with croquet clubs and the one golf ball we owned.

I should mention that getting to the creek sometimes involved a little danger since the shortcut I chose involved climbing a barbed wire fence. Mom once caught me in the act and yelled at me, startling me so that I jumped, tearing open the skin of one knee. It took weeks to heal and left a large, noticeable scar that I wore as a badge of honor for years. I still climbed that fence when I was in a hurry and no one was looking. I can't find the scar now and don't remember which knee was injured.

Once when the first crop had been cleared from the two-acre field left of the house, a host of milkweeds sprang up. My father offered my sister and me a penny for each one we pulled up. We tried but soon found our hands sticky and the heat oppressive. That "get rich scheme" went by the boards. Years later Dad made a tennis court for us on a part of that field near the house. He was meticulous about following the rules for building it, but it was not a success. The ground was not hard enough for the ball to bounce properly.

Our home looked like a square box, slightly longer than it was wide. There was a large living room. Alongside it at the front was a room that was never sure what it was: sometimes a dining room, sometimes a place where we put things we didn't know what to do with, but always a front exit. It held my father's desk and a settee where we children (by then I had a little sister) sat to change footwear~rubbers, galoshes, shoes and tennis shoes (nobody called them sneakers!)~and it was there that I learned right and left. For years I would envision myself on that bench to make sure left was really left and right was really right.

The living room itself was nondescript until my mother happened upon a sale of Early American maple furniture and rag carpeting. Our piano was there, as well as a bookcase. It was an attractive room, but we used it only on special occasions. I had to go in to practice on the piano and on Saturdays to clean. The latter generally ended with my mother scolding me for reading instead of dusting. During the winters we lived in the "little room" off the kitchen where an open wood-burning stove had been installed. In the summers we lived on the roomy screened-in back porch.

Upstairs there were four bedrooms and a bath. They were square boxy rooms except for the one on the northeast, smaller because it was what was left when Dad put in the bath. That room was the coziest and became my sister's. The southwest one always belonged to my parents. I generally liked the northwest room. It gave me plenty of space for my books and the walking sticks and stones I collected on family outings.

The remaining room on the southeast was for guests. In my fifth year I was put to bed in that room one afternoon for a nap. It was still light outside. When my mother woke me, I sat up and looked at the window: it was dark. I had wasted my day. I broke into tears and cried, "I'm sleeping my life away!"

All the rooms were wall-papered, bright and cheerful patterns, always renewed if they became worn or soiled. Cleaning was achieved with a malleable substance, bright pink in color and pleasant smelling. It came in a can, was kneaded into a ball and used to wipe every inch of the wallpaper, gradually turning black as it absorbed the dirt. Even kids could do this boring job, and we rarely escaped. In the basement there was a large coal-burning furnace which heated the house. My sister and I loved to stand over the one big register on the first floor and feel our dresses swirl out when the heat was coming up strongly.

But I have digressed from an orderly account of my life. When I was two and a half, I learned I had a little sister. It was then customary not to tell children another child was expected. I was obviously not an observant kid and did not notice Mom was getting fat. I have always been told that I went and found my special blanket and handed it over for her. I view this story with suspicion, doubtful about such generosity toward a little person I had just met and didn't know.

I was born Margaret Aileene, my sister Lucile Idell. Parents should be required to take a course entitled "The Proper Naming of Children." The fact that Lu's name was spelled with only one "l" required her to be vigilant her whole life to make sure it was correct. And I thought my middle name was affected and never used it, though I might have had it not had a final "e." Dad called us Margaret and Lucile; Mom called us Maggie Sue and Peggy Lu. Each of us shortened her name or used a nickname.

Lu was beautiful, with a generally cheerful disposition. I was plain with a mercurial disposition. Once the tonsils were gone, I had good health. There were no vaccines to protect against childhood diseases, so we caught whatever came around. I was usually only a little sick, while Lu often became seriously ill. To

2.2 Lu at three

make things worse, her pony, on a gallop, stepped into a hole and she was thrown. Three major bones were broken, and she spent the next months in a rigid cast. She never rode again. Then came whooping cough, dangerous for the 1920's child. I remember her thin and white, falling to the floor from coughing. She might have died had it not been for the skill and devotion of our mother. Barely through that ordeal, she caught scarlet fever and was quarantined and bedridden for weeks.

Lu bounced back, full of wit, humor and mischief. For dessert one evening, she and I were serving slices of ice cream on plates. As I followed her down the passage from kitchen to dining room, I saw ice cream on the floor. Mom, following me, called out, "Who spilled the ice cream?" Before I could collect my wits, Lu answered, "Maggie did." It was a never-ending family argument, Lu dying without ever confessing her guilt.

Lu's favorite color was blue, mine red. One Easter we were outfitted with hats, each in her favorite color. Those were the only hats we owned. During the summer there was a death in an older family in town, friends of our parents. Neither of them could attend the funeral, so Lu and I were sent. It would have been unthinkable to go bareheaded, but we suffered acute embarrassment in our unorthodox headgear at such a solemn affair.

When I was four or five, my sister and I were taken on a shopping trip to Medina, the country seat seven miles away. This was customary; if you went somewhere, you took the kids. As Mom browsed the aisles of a "dry goods" store, Lu and I were at liberty to roam. I passed a table laden with handkerchiefs: white with small, colorful flowers embroidered in the corners. Without thinking or hesitation, I stuffed a handful of them into my coat pocket. I must have known I had done wrong because I felt uneasy,[1] and as soon as we arrived home, I went to my room, quickly shoved them into the top drawer of my dresser, got undressed and climbed into bed. It was late and my mother came in to straighten up the room and open the window. I heard her pulling out that drawer. Without a word, she left and minutes later my father called, "Margaret, come down here, please." He didn't sound angry, but that didn't lessen my anxiety. He took me on his lap and talked to me about how taking things that don't belong to you is stealing, and stealing is wrong, then sent me back to bed, saying they would help me make the matter right. When next we were in Medina,

---

1   This is in line with recent thinking that even babies have a moral sense. See *New York Times Magazine*, 5/8/10.

we went back to the store. I asked for the manager, gave back the handkerchiefs, and said I was sorry. It was hard, but I do not believe I have since stolen anything more than a very few books and some pink pencils, the latter something I have to admit because there was a witness. When Mindy was seven or eight, I used to employ her to do filing in my office on Saturdays and school holidays. She was paid 50 cents an hour out of my pocket and worth every penny. One such day she happened to be looking in my desk drawer and exclaimed, "Here's where the pink pencils come from!" My boss at that moment was walking by. I thought his smile was somewhat rueful. Neither of us ever mentioned the incident.

Early on, probably five or six, I went with my parents to a fund-raising dinner at a hotel in the Chippewa amusement park, usually used only in the summer when the park was open. Dad was a member of the American Legion, an organization of veterans. Mom and Dad were on the committee and involved in preparing and serving the food, so the kitchen was where Lu and I played. I discovered that under one of the huge tables was a cache of small barrels and in one of those were~olives! the delicious kind with red stuffing. I spent the rest of the evening under that table. An acquired taste? Nonsense. Just make them available. Should I say I got sick and never wanted another olive? Again nonsense. I didn't get sick and to this day I love olives.

When I was six, I started school. Chippewa Lake had its own elementary school in a two-room building set far back on a large lot on the main road connecting the town with Route 3, the highway running from Cleveland to Columbus to Cincinnati. There was a fence of single iron bars across the front of the lot on which, if you were daring, you could do acrobatics. The big children used the large front yard for ball, hopscotch, tag and other games they fancied, and there was a playground in the rear with swings, seesaws, a merry-go-round and slides for the younger children. There were two outdoor toilets. The building was heated by a large, round furnace in the middle of each room. There was a woman teacher in the "little room" and a man in the "big room." The school was about a mile from our home, and we walked there and back in all weathers. There was no bus.

2.3 Chippewa Lake School, first four grades

Near the end of my first year of school, with the coming of spring, three other first grade girls and I used to go to a small grove of trees next to the playground, paper bags in hand, for lunch. Our first move was to strip off shoes and socks and enjoy the cool ground. A girl who was not a special friend reported to the teacher that we were "showing our bloomers," a brazen lie. Suddenly one day, all the fun was interrupted by grown-ups. We were scolded, herded into school, made to kneel on the seats of our desks, paddled by our teacher and sent home in disgrace. At no point were we told what we were being disciplined for, nor were we allowed to defend ourselves. At home I was punished again, this time with a peach tree sprout. I remember the dreadful wait while my mother went out to find and

SCHOOL YEAR 1925-26															Dorothy Kundig Teacher	
Month	Conduct	Application	Spelling	Reading	Writing	Arithmetic	Language Grammar	Geography	History	Physiology	Civics	Drawing	Music	Agriculture	Man. Training Dom. Science	Weight	Monthly Average
1st	G	E		E	E	E										5/4 47	
2nd	E	E		E	E	E										52	
3rd	E	E		E	E	E										48 3/4	
4th	E	E		a	E	a										49	
5th	E	E	a	a	E+	a	a									82 52	
6th	E	E	a	a	E+	a	a									53 52	
7th	E	E	a	a	a	a										53	
8th	E	E	a	a	a	a										54	
9th	E	E	a	a	a	a										55	
1st Semester Average																	
2nd Semester Average																	
Yearly Average																	

This Certifies That Margret Browns

18 { Retained in { Promoted to {   Grade Second

L. E. Pickham Supt.

2.5 Maggie's first grade report card

cut a suitable one. It stung. My friend Eileen Reese was also whipped again, she with a fly swatter.

Lu and I started out playing together but our interests diverged. She liked dolls; I held a funeral service one summer day and buried the beautiful, expensive doll received the previous Christmas. I liked riding; she never rode again after her accident. I liked the creek; she found it cold and lonesome. I liked the lake; she was often happy to go just once a day. She was a champion Monopoly player; I found it impossible to beat her, so why try? I remember we did enjoy Hearts and were fortunate to have a card table with room between the rim and the top so you could use it to line up all the 13 cards our hands were not big enough to hold.

Dad being a veteran, we always went to the Memorial Day parade in Medina, despite his having more difficulty every year getting into his uniform. I shall always remember how beautiful the irises were, in full bloom every year on that day. As a member of the American Legion, he also participated in the sale of poppies for the care of disabled vets. I was the one delegated to go house-to-house selling them for 10 cents each. Knocking on all those strange doors was terrifying, and a lot of the time I was refused, dimes being hard to come by in those days. But l was called to go, and I stayed out until every last one was sold.

From time to time our Methodist Church would import an evangelist for a night or two. It was the big show in town when it happened, and every man and his brother, along with their wives and kids, would attend. One year when I was about 10, the speaker was so persuasive in calling sinners to the altar to be saved, that I was moved to join them. But when I got to the altar, every inch of space was already occupied by a repentant sinner; there was no room for me. I went back and sat down and never did get saved.

We visited each set of grandparents every year. Each was about 200 miles from our home (in opposite directions), long and difficult trips, especially since we never could afford a new car or one of a better make, having graduated from Model T's to Model A's to various used cars and eventually to a succession of Willys. Seldom did we make the trip without a breakdown, and it was customary, once we arrived, for relatives with a bent for auto repair to "tear down" the car and only manage to put it back together by the time we were to leave.

When my sister and I visited our grandparents Brown, they seemed happy to see us, but made little fuss and few efforts to entertain us. What we remembered most was that their well water contained sulphur, making it smell like rotten eggs, and that our grandmother had made pancakes for her family every single day of her marriage, some 30 or more years. Our visits to our grandparents Hall were more festive. They lived on a cattle farm. A pony and cart were hitched up for us to drive, behind the house there was a fascinating, wonderfully cool cave-like structure to explore where food was kept, and fireplaces, and cousins to meet from the first marriages of both grandparents. And it was there I first discovered the Tarzan books I immediately loved.

Poison ivy was the bane of my young life. Every summer I was purple for weeks, the result of being painted with potassium permanganate to fight the unbearable itch.

While I was in the lower grades, two of our teachers organized a Girl Scout troop. I remember having trouble starting a fire without matches; I remember Smores;[2] I remember we were given a project: to plan three meals for six people on $6.00; and I learned one knot that has stayed with me and proven to be the only one anyone (except sailors) ever needs: right over left and left over right.

I also remember a fateful day in 1933–I now know it was in March –when President Franklin D. Roosevelt closed the banks, and our Scout leaders were left wondering how they would manage without funds. No one I knew was panicking, there seemed to be a feeling of confidence, and it was apparently that move and others that saved the banking system from collapse. Later we saw the government provide jobs to some of the unemployed in town, and the son of a neighbor, out of work, joined the CCC (Civilian Conservation Corps) and went to plant trees and otherwise take care of the forests, developing new methods of fighting forest fires. But in FDR's first week, Hitler came to power, and I was still a school girl when we learned about Mussolini invading Ethiopia and Germany the Rhineland, and how

---

2   Marshmallows toasted over an open fire and served between graham crackers with the addition of a square of milk chocolate. Unforgettable.

both of them were soon fighting in Spain. Looking back, I realize that FDR never had a day in office when he did not have to fight fascism.

We knew times were tough when every so often a homeless man would knock on our door, desperate for food. We were off the beaten path, so it did not happen often, but when it did, Mom would not hesitate. She would give him soap and a towel and point out the pump in the middle of the yard. She would offer a cold drink and cool place to wait or a hot drink and a warm place to wait, depending on the weather. She would then immediately start to make him a meal. If it was near our mealtime, she would share our food; if not, she could always make him a nutritious dinner starting with eggs and bacon or the home-canned sausage always available, plus all the trimmings. She would also engage him in conversation and send him on encouraged. She always reached out, too, to the minister of the Brethren Church and his family. His parishioners were not as well off as the Methodists. Mom sometimes found them in almost desperate circumstances but uncomplaining.

Besides Eileen Reese, who had been with me when we were spanked in school, I had another friend, Fern Derhammer. The three of us went from first grade through high school together, always in friendly competition. Eileen's father was a telegraph operator on the B&O Railroad, and her parents and mine were friends. Fern's father was a farmer with a stand of sugar maples. In early spring, while the snow was still on the ground, Mr. Derhammer, in his horse-pulled cart, would empty the pails hanging on the trees and take the sap to a shed. Then, the sap would be boiled on a hot stove until it became thick. Upon cooling, it changed color and solidified into cakes. We were given hot syrup that we poured on pans of snow until it was cold enough to eat. It was delicious, and we repeated that process all day. I paid: for several days after that I could eat nothing but grapefruit. Sadly, Mr. Derhammer was killed by lightning in 1936. He had taken refuge under a tree during a sudden summer storm.

The competition among Fern, Eileen and me was constant. The rivalry never seemed to cause any hard feelings. In high school another friend was added, Mildred Jones. Of the four of us, I was the only one afforded a chance to go to college, although all the others were at least as able as I. I owe my mother a major debt for that. The famous mother from *I Remember Mama* had nothing on my Mom. She always made sure she had as much income of her own as she could earn, and she saved what she could from her weekly household allowance, so when I was ready for college there was a small nest egg to get started. After that, it often happened that when a tuition payment was due, there would be a calf old enough to sell. Mom's steadfast conviction that girls should be educated continued with Lu who, after high school, was enrolled in a 4-year nursing program for a B.S. and an R.N.

My parents consistently sought to broaden our lives. We were taken to the movies whenever we were in Medina on a Saturday night. It was always a Western. You could tell the good guys by their white hats. We went to Lodi to see Katharine Hepburn in *Little Women* in 1934. That same year we went to Cleveland for the Barnum & Bailey circus. The circus was not in a tent but in the Coliseum. I could not enjoy it for worrying that the high ceiling, without anything to support it, would collapse on us. On top of that, while we were watching a high wire act only about 15 feet above the floor, without a net, the woman performing on it suddenly lost her footing and fell, hitting the floor in a flash. It was quickly obvious her neck was broken. No emergency crew came to help her. Her body was covered with a blanket and taken away. On a happier day in 1939 we went to Cleveland again to see *Gone With the Wind*, cheerfully waiting in lines that went around the block.

Every summer we toured Ohio to see historic places, caverns, waterfalls, Indian mounds, a salt mine, a Blue Hole reputed to have no bottom. Two summers we spent time in Michigan, camping on a lake, swimming and fishing. I got lost twice: once, on disembarking from a huge sightseeing boat on Lake Michigan, I found myself surrounded by hundreds of strangers and our parents nowhere in sight; second, our parents awoke to find that Lu and I had left the cottage, untied a rowboat and drifted onto the lake, fortunately not yet so far from shore that we could not be rescued. What I remember most, however, was a visit to a Ford factory where I was overwhelmed by the noise and heat and the sight of the men working and sweating in it, air conditioning not having been invented.

I was subject to tonsillitis. Almost every birthday I spent in bed with a painful throat. When I was 8, my parents decided enough was enough, and my tonsils and adenoids were removed at Wadsworth Hospital. The bill for the operation and the hospital stay was $35. I was promised ice cream if I was good. When it came, I could not eat it, of course, and cried bitterly at life's unfairness. In spite of my annual illness, I remember we always had modest but magical Christmases. One year there was very little money; by making our dresses and play clothes, my mother managed to clothe my sister and me, including shoes, for a total of $5 for the year; but there was little extra money for presents. Dad built a small barn he painted gray and a small table he painted red. For a few cents, Mom bought celluloid farm animals for the barn and metal dishes for the table. We played happily with them for years.

My parents were hard-working and frugal. We never had to buy food except for oranges, bananas, sugar, coffee, tea, salt, spices, raisins, margarine (the latter arriving in an off-putting white color it was my job to turn to a more or less inviting yellow) and bread. Mom refused to bake the last item though she made cakes, cookies, pies, biscuits, dumplings, and later, under the baker's tutelage, delicious pecan rolls. She also made our butter and cottage cheese. The garden produced every imaginable vegetable, starting in the spring with asparagus and rhubarb, continuing through the summer with strawberries, cherries, corn, beans, lettuce, tomatoes, squash, watermelons and cantaloupes and ending with the winter's supply of potatoes. The orchard provided a variety of peaches and apples, and later honey. The surrounding countryside offered blackberries, elderberries, black walnuts, and hickory nuts. As to meat, Mom raised chickens and Dad raised a young pig to be butchered in the fall and yearly bought a quarter of beef. Everything cannable was canned; everything freezable was frozen; everything that could be jellied or jammed was.

Many years there would be a fall day when the house was buzzing with activity earlier than usual. There would be a neighbor woman sitting in our kitchen, running an apple-peeler at full speed, and outside, in the large open space in front of our barn, there would be a huge copper kettle suspended over a fire. It had a long arm so that one could stand about 10 feet away and stir the contents of the kettle. This cooking went on for hours, and finally Mom would officiate at putting in the proper seasoning. I remember she used spicy hard red candies to give it a distinctive and delicious flavor. Then the apple butter would be labeled into jars, with everyone who had helped receiving a generous share, and the copper kettle would disappear to wherever it had come from.

If we ran out of some essential, it might perhaps be found in the local store, but serious grocery shopping was done periodically in Medina, seven miles away, and if we had eggs to sell, that's also where we took them. The foray I remember best took place on a Saturday night in the dead of winter after a deep snowfall. We traveled in a horse-drawn open sleigh with the egg crate tied on the back. We were able to enjoy sleigh rides whenever there was enough snow because Dad was always on the lookout for sleighs the farmers on his route no longer wanted and were pleased to sell or give away. As a result, if one sleigh wore out, we always had another in the wings. On another of these trips to Medina we visited "Doc" Robinson, a licensed physician respected by my mother. He examined all four of us, prescribed and furnished whatever pills he advised, and charged a total of $3.00.

We had no newspapers~too costly. There was a telephone, a large oaken box on the wall offering a party line, but it lasted only a year~too costly. Dad saw the papers at work and daily regaled us with the latest wise and witty saying by Will Rogers, but we were shielded from most of the news. There was heavy unemployment and there were families in town on relief, but Dad had a job. It paid only $200 a month, but our thrifty, innovative parents managed. I heard the word "Hoovervilles," huge tent cities of the homeless unemployed, but never saw one. We heard about a government program to hire the unemployed. It was called the WPA. There was also something called the PWA. I found these confusing.[3] I remember hearing about

3   I now know that the WPA was the Works Progress Administration, its name being changed in 1939 to the Works Projects Administration. It was a government program that provided jobs for almost 8 million unemployed, constructing public buildings and roads, operating programs in the arts, feeding children and redistriibuting food, clothing and housing. The PWA, the Works Projects Administration, was also a huge government operation started in 1933. It contracted with private construction companies to build dams and bridges. It did not hire the unemployed directly but instead hired on the open market.

John L. Lewis, the birth of the Congress of Industrial Organizations (CIO) and the desperate sit-down strikes, but I was more bewildered and frightened by those events than understanding of them. Dad, who was born and raised a Republican, voted for FDR; Mom, a born Democrat, cancelled his vote by supporting the Republican, Alf Landon. As far as I know, they followed that pattern all their lives.

Once a year we were taken to the Chippewa Lake Amusement Park where we could ride the merry-go-round, the Ferris wheel and, if we dared, the roller coaster. I dared only once. We always went to the Medina County Fair. One year I rode my pony in the pony race. We had misjudged it. I was the only girl and my pony the only small one. All the boys had big ponies and it shocked me to see how they whipped them. Halfway through, I saw I was nowhere near finishing with the others. There was an opening in the fence so I simply rode through it and went the seven miles home. My parents did not know where I was but had the good sense not to worry.

My folks had chosen to attend the Methodist Church, the more prestigious of the two churches in town. They went on high days and holidays, but we kids were expected to attend every Sunday. One Sunday I announced I was not going. Lu went off on time. I sat on the second-floor steps, halfway to the top, and could hear Mom complaining to Dad, "I just don't know what I'm going to do with that child. She's out of control," and ending with a decision that I must be punished. I was out of there and on my way to Sunday School before you could blink. That was the closest I came to rebellion and it lasted about a minute and a half.

Every year, as soon as the weather broke, I began going barefoot from the first day of vacation to the last. Sundays were always a problem, it being necessary to wear shoes to Sunday School. I remember two summers when I unintentionally solved that problem by breaking a toe (both times in a night-time rush to the bathroom involving a collision of a little toe with a doorjamb, making it impossible to wear shoes for weeks and weeks). One year when I failed to have an excuse, I had to attend Bible School at the Methodist Church for several weeks. My report card was filled with golden harps and other heavenly signs of perfect attendance and expertise at learning Bible verses,

Only two of literally dozens of sermons I must have sat through remain with me. In one, the minister talked of co-operation, emphasizing and repeating it endlessly. I now guess he was having his problems, but then I couldn't wait for the service to end so I could speak to Mom. She had told me what an operation was but had never explained co-operation. The other sermon involved Ben Hur, saying that one could profit from it in three ways, by enjoying the story including the fabulous chariot race; by learning the history of the times; and by having one's faith shored up by Jesus' miracles.

Our church was not rich. But if it needed to raise $100 or $500, this is what I saw happen time and again. One parishioner, a prosperous older farmer, would get to his feet and say "I'll give half that amount if the rest of you will raise the balance." Hands would start to go up and pledges of $10 and $20 would come in until the total was reached. The devotion of the farmer was unfailing, and his psychology was superb.

I remember waking up one Saturday morning when I was about seven or eight to hear my father calling, "Margaret, come down. Your little 'darky' friend has come to see you." I knew that little kid slightly. His family, the only black[4] folks in town, had just moved to Chippewa. Even I could see he was lonesome. He had walked me home one day after school. So I knew why he had come to visit but I knew from the way my Dad sounded that he disapproved. I was totally intimidated and did not go down, something I have regretted ever since. That was the only black family ever to live in Chippewa, as far as I know. They stayed only a few weeks. There were no Jewish families.

When I was about nine or ten, I learned from the local beauty parlor that it was possible to have a haircut called a "boyish bob." I discussed and debated it for so long, my mother finally said in exasperation, "Have it or don't have it, but for goodness sake, don't talk about it any more." I had it and for six weeks looked like a boy.

On July 6, 1932 Dad took me to the post office to be part of a history-making day: first class postage went from two to three cents. Except for a brief period during World War I, the two-cent rate had

4   I have lived through a variety of ways of speaking of people of color. They were called Colored, then Negroes, then Black and now African American. I like the last but find it ponderous and have decided therefore to simply use "black" through all the historical periods I mention.

lasted almost 50 years! I am trying to become a stamp collector and have learned that a great age of stamps followed with FDR and James A. Farley as his Postmaster General, both being avid collectors.

In January 1935, I was notified that I was first in History, Latin II and Geometry in the Ohio Every Pupil Tests. It was no big deal. No bells rang, no rewards were offered. But I was pleased.

Two months later, I was in the bathroom when I looked out the window and saw that the roof was lightly covered with snow but was also on fire.[5] I screamed and ran downstairs. Dad was at work. Mom was needed at home. There was no one to go for the volunteer fire department but me. I started out on the family bike to go the half-mile to town. We lived on a macadam road. It was considered "improved," having been constructed in such fashion that the dirt was very compacted and covered with gray-blue stones. It was almost impossible for bike riding since the cars would throw the stones into small hills on each side, forcing the bike rider to use the middle of the road and to stop and climb up on the stones if a car approached. There were no cars that morning but the trip seemed never to end. As I approached the top of the hill just before town I remember getting off the bike and running, pushing it as I went. As soon as I got to town I stood in the middle of the street and yelled at the top of my lungs, over and over, "Our house is on fire! Call the fire department!"

The men in the fire department came together from wherever they were working and put out the fire. The bike and I made it home and later that very day we went to Medina to buy a new roof. We were euphoric: our house was not badly damaged, all our things were safe, no one was injured, and we were unanimously in agreement that the new roof should be red. The fire, started by a spark from the chimney, turned out to cost $150, even with my father putting on the new roof.

My father was always seeking ways to supplement our income. He tried raising bees. Lu and I got particular joy from seeing him work with them, protected by his wide-brimmed hat with a metal mesh veil, long, thick gloves and a device that burned rags and emitted puffs of smoke. I never knew if he made any money selling honey but he needed the bees anyway for the orchard.

---

5   My diary, March 9, 1935.

Next he undertook to run a dairy: he modernized the barn with stalls for the cows, even individual drinking bowls; he bought more Jerseys because he liked the 5% butter fat milk they give; he built a small building and installed equipment for sterilizing milk bottles; he designed and ordered Willowdale bottles; he acquired a delivery cart to be pulled by our horse; and he went into business. Every morning he would waken one of us girls to accompany him on the route. We would ride on the back of the cart, run up to the house, put down the order, pick up the empties, and run back. The end of the run was always the bakery, where an excellent baker presided. The gossip was that he was an alcoholic and his wife had insisted they move to a village without a tavern. Whatever the reason, it was the town's luck to have him and whoever had worked the delivery that morning was likely to have a treat.

Lu and I were expected to do some work but my mother's philosophy was that we would have plenty of work to do when we were grown, so she wanted us to have as much leisure as possible while we were children. Our tasks were never too arduous. There being no son and I being the elder, I was assigned to help Dad while Lu helped Mom. I had chores like throwing down hay from the second floor of the barn for the horses and cows, feeding the chickens, feeding the pig if there was one (a piglet being purchased every year and raised until fall when it was slaughtered), etc. One of the results of this arrangement was that Lu became a good cook while I did not. I did, however, become the family cake baker, my specialty being angel food. Both of us were on the cleanup detail for dishes after dinner, cleaning our rooms weekly and running the milk bottles every other day. My chores were increased to include washing the milk bottles daily and stacking them in the sterilizer.

I should add that Mom's philosophy about not making us work too hard was not the whole story. She frequently quoted (I never knew the source): "Lost, somewhere between sunrise and sunset, 60 golden minutes, each set with 60 diamond seconds. No reward is offered for they are gone forever." We were not to forget that life is short and time is fleeting. Use it; don't waste it!

Chippewa actually had a lake. It had been made by damming up the outlet while leaving the inlet untouched. About a mile long, it was then and, as I observed on a recent trip back, still is quite beautiful. The east side was developed with cottages, well built and cared for, many used year-round. The amusement park was also well cared for and not gaudy. The west side was farmland, green and lovely. The lake was also a mile wide from east to west; I know because I swam it on July 14, 1935, Dad accompanying me in a rowboat.

Because of the lake, people from Cleveland, 35 miles away, found it convenient for vacationing. There were cottages for rent, and in lean years my mother took in summer boarders. Most of them were nice

2.5 Maggie after swimming the lake

friendly people who enjoyed the country~swimming, berry picking, riding, helping with the hay season. Some came back the next year; a few became and remained friends. In this category were an engineer and his wife from Cleveland. He was a longtime employee of GE and told us that even then GE knew how to manufacture a really long-lived electric light bulb but was withholding it from the market for profit reasons.

We also met and got to know some of the cottagers. One summer I organized the summer kids and one or two of my friends to put on a play. Our version of Tom Sawyer and Huck Finn was something to behold. All the grownups came. The cemetery scene became the high point of the evening. As Tom twirled him around, our cat, playing the role of the dead feline, suddenly went out of character, yowled alarmingly and exited precipitously. Part of my teenage years was spent mooning over one boy whose name was Junior Wiebusch. The last time I saw him he came to say goodbye. It was 1940 and he was going to Canada to join the Royal Canadian Air Force in order to get to England to fight the Nazis. There was reputed to be a 90% fatality rate in that outfit. I never heard from him again.

I reveled in the lake, walking over every morning and every afternoon to swim or sunbathe. As often as he could my father would accompany my sister and me for a swim in the evening, Mom's health not permitting her to swim. I remember one day when I went to the lake alone three times--before breakfast, before lunch, before dinner and then after dark with Dad and Lu! And then there was the time my mother made a deal with a voice teacher who lived a block from the lake: I was to teach her two young sons to swim and in return receive singing lessons. Since her usual charge for a lesson was $1.00, that was a deal one could not refuse (assuming one wanted voice lessons, which I did not). The kids got to the point where they could be trusted not to drown; I never got that far with the voice lessons.

One year there was a diving contest at the lake. In preparation, a tall diving platform was built on the shore. I went to the lake very early the next day and was surprised to see it. There was not a soul but myself anywhere in sight. In legal terms, this constituted an "attractive nuisance," a situation appealing to the young and holding the possibility of danger. What did I do? Climbed to the top immediately. Once there, I had my very first attack of acrophobia, leaving me completely paralyzed. I simply could not move. After a long while, I realized I had no idea when help would come—I had to rely on myself. The climb down took three or four times longer and was no fun at all. To this day, I avoid heights. When I am forced to go to the top of a tall building and look down, I hold on *very* tightly.

My parents decided my shyness had to be treated. They took me to Medina to an elocution teacher, Miss Tibbetts. I was taught to recite poetry, tell stories and declaim orations breathing from the diaphragm--or was that singing lessons? Then I was signed up for the Prince of Peace competition organized by the Ohio Council of Churches, reacting to World War I and attempting to build a peace movement. Each year a new booklet of speeches was issued. I had to choose one, learn it, give it any number of times when some organization needed a speaker free of charge--our church, an American Legion meeting, anywhere else I was invited, and finally in the county contest. One year I won that contest with a piece entitled "We Who Are About To Die Salute You." I was then required to compete in the district contest, where I lost to a boy. Miss Tibbetts nevertheless rewarded me by taking me to Cleveland to see Leslie Howard in *Hamlet*.

At 13 I learned to drive a car but could not obtain a license until 16. I practiced on our driveway, going forward until I reached the road and then backing up until I returned to the barn. And doing it over and over and over. I became a good backer. On my 16th birthday I went for the license. No exam was required.

I was a child of little musical talent, but my parents were wedded to my having a musical education. My father's piano playing was limited, so limited in fact that he could play only one song, "The Old Rugged Cross." He played it perfectly a few times a year for many years, never showing the least desire to increase his repertoire. He had a pleasant baritone voice and sang well. Mom loved music, did not play an instrument, liked to sing and could not carry a tune.

I suffered through several years of lessons on the piano, starting early with a young woman who charged 50 cents a lesson. She was the daughter of a well-to-do farmer and was in college. That she was earning some money was a sign of the family's frugality; that she could charge so little was a sign of how bad the times were. I hated to practice and avoided it as often as possible. There was one exception. When we had a summer thunderstorm~and we often did~I played the piano as loudly as I could to shut out the noise for as long as the storm lasted.

I did become skilled enough to take part in a county-wide contest where I came in second. I might have been first, but at the last minute I chickened out on performing without the music, carrying it with me to the piano. I didn't need it and played without a mistake, but having taken the music counted against me. Whenever the Methodist Church pianist failed to show up, I was asked to play. I was never warned and therefore not prepared and usually stumbled through.

The piano lessons were followed by~excruciating thought!~several years of misbegotten violin lessons about which it is the better part of valor to remain silent. I should add that Lu achieved much more success on that instrument. As to vocal music, I was an alto, sang in a high school trio where my favorite was "Ave Maria" and a chorus that went to New York City to demonstrate the visionary music program developed by Medina County. I came home with the measles.

Medina County prided itself on other advanced educational practices. Every school had weekly visits from an art teacher and a music teacher. Later, a yearly program was introduced to test every student's vision. This played a crucial role in my life. For years I had been moved closer and closer to the blackboard until finally, by the time I reached the big room, I was on the platform with the teacher's desk. It was found that I was very near-sighted. Given glasses, I was surprised to see that the leaves on the trees had definite shapes, they were not just a blur of green. I went home that night, got on my pony and rode and rode, crying my eyes out at the thought that I would have to wear glasses all the time and boys would never look at me but realizing that it was good to see the leaves and the blackboard and all I had been missing.

All this happened almost 80 years ago. While I was writing this in 2011, I heard of a town in my state which has cancelled all music and art programs in its schools. One cannot help but be struck by what a backward step this is! And one wonders just what other services needed by the children are also being eliminated, and worries at how fast this penny-pinching at the expense of the most vulnerable is spreading to other schools in the nation.

When I was 13 and in the 8th grade, I suddenly found to my horror that I was bleeding. I was then a very religious girl. I didn't tell Mom about my problem. I told God, sincerely and at length, pleading on my knees to be allowed to live. I was saved by my mother's discovery of my plight.

I liked to read. We had no public library and books were too expensive to buy. Whenever I could, I expropriated them (exception to the no-stealing rule). Besides the childhood classics, I was able to read *Microbe Hunters* (I resolved to be a scientist), a volume of Sholem Aleichem's stories (I was preordained to like Jews), and as many Tarzan books as I could get my hands on.

We always had ponies, horses and pets. We had house cats and barn cats, the latter not allowed in the house because they were working cats whose job it was to kill rats. After eating rats for a period, they would sicken and die. We always had a dog, the one we remembered best being Heidi, a white shepherd. She had been bumped by a car when a puppy and thereafter chased cars. She was killed by one on April 8, 1934. We got our first ponies on loan for the off-season from the circus. Mine was Bob and Lu's was Bill. Bob liked to run; Bill was fat and lazy. At the end of the term, Bill went back but Bob had lost sight in one eye and the circus no longer wanted him. I could enjoy him until one sad day in April, 1934 when we had to sell him. I do not know why; we may not have been able to feed him. In the years that followed, I always had a horse, Sally Forth being the one I remember best.

My diary notes in January, 1934, "Mother getting well. B.C. up from 52 to 85 in 4 weeks. Isn't Dr. Southwick wonderful?" Mom had been an invalid for some years, starting with the scarlet fever through which she nursed Lu. Mom loved nursing and always conducted herself on the highest professional level, with the result that I witnessed the following: She did not normally work outside the home, but whenever either Dr. Robinson in Medina or Dr. Beach in Seville had a gravely ill patient, he would call on Mom, trusting there was no one in the county more skilled or dedicated. Mom would appear in her starched white uniform with her Biltmore Hospital pin and cap and we would be in awe. There was an additional indication of the trust in which she was held by the medical profession. When Lu came down with contagious scarlet fever while we were running a dairy, Mom was trusted to manage things in such a way that no one else would be infected. No one was. But when the danger of an epidemic was over, Mom herself came down with the disease.

It was almost a death sentence, coming on top of the serious chronic conditions she already had. We had many nights when we thought she was going to die. She was totally incapacitated and we had to have a "hired girl." By this time, Dad was working his job, running the farm and the dairy, helping to take care of Mom and us and going to law school three nights a week. We obviously also had to have a "hired man." One of those "hired men" was George Richie. He was a young man who, just out of high school and planning to go to college, was involved in a terrible auto accident that put an end to any such hopes because, by the time he was well, all the money was gone. He was not long with us before he was accepted by both my parents as the son they never had and idolized as a big brother by Lu and me. Our hired girl took quite a liking to him, but he did not reciprocate. Later on, after we no longer employed him and he moved on, he continued to visit us. I adored him for many years, but I was too young and too unsophisticated to interest him.

D. M. Brown

2.6 Dad graduating from law school

Dad was graduated from Akron Law School in June of 1936, but by then the State of Ohio had passed a law requiring a bachelor's degree in order to take the bar.

One of the features of living in a small town is that there are few secrets. That was true in Chippewa. Whatever happened soon became general knowledge, even among the children. We were growing up during the Great Depression and one of its offshoots was a high incidence of suicides. I remember three, two involving men and one involving a couple. The last was called a double suicide but there was talk around town about whether it could have been a murder and a suicide. Because everyone knew everyone else, the whole town was stricken, not just for days, but for weeks. I do not believe it was working people involved but rather men whose businesses had failed. My dear friend in high school lost her father to suicide for such a reason. The sadness of that experience was with her all her life.

There was one couple in town who lived the high life. He drank and she was a bottle blonde, always heavily made up and dressed to kill. The rumor was that they neglected their two young daughters. Suddenly we heard they had "got religion." We never knew from whence; I'm pretty sure it wasn't either the Methodists or the Brethren.

They rented or bought a corner store on the main street and turned it into a grocery and general store. He became post master, with the post office occupying a corner of the store. I was shocked to see her —brown hair, no makeup, housedress, waiting on customers. To the best of my knowledge there was no relapse; the cure was complete.

On another occasion there was talk about town that Mr. G, the older, married teacher in the "big room," was having an affair with Miss K, the young, unmarried teacher in the "little room." The evidence? They had locked the children out one afternoon. My parents were outraged at the story and took steps to find out the truth. The building was locked on only one occasion, when the teachers were putting up decorations for a surprise Halloween party for the children. The whole community knew both teachers to be people of integrity and high standards, but if such gossip were permitted to go unchecked, the Board of Education would have no choice but to fire them. Mom and Dad wasted no time. They went to see the families of the teachers to reassure them of support and then visited the most upright of the Methodists and enlisted their help in reaching influential families with children in school. Mom had a good relationship with the minister of the Brethren Church, who agreed to speak to his parishioners. Dad, going round his mail route, had a perfect opportunity to combat the scandal and spread the truth. Tragedy was averted, and faith restored.

By the time I reached the 8th grade, my father, with Mom's encouragement, had become president of the Board of Education. They were determined the 8th grade would not be the end of our schooling. He led the Board in making a contract with Westfield High School three miles away in LeRoy, a picture-pretty town practically owned lock, stock and barrel by a company, to the best of my recollection, The Ohio Farmers' Insurance Company. Even every blade of grass behaved itself. The school was a revelation to us when we visited it for the first time~modern, handsome, in perfect repair. And we were to be bussed there and back!

As graduation loomed, I had my first lesson in politics. The class met to pick colors. I favored yellow and something else. I lost. The opposition had already made a decision and carried the day. However, on graduation night—May 25, 1937—I was the yellow organdy in the sea of white.

III
LEROY, NEW CONCORD
AND CHARLOTTE
(1933-1943)

The next four years were spent at Westfield High School in LeRoy. I had trouble with algebra. I was good in geometry. I somehow avoided cooking but had to take sewing and survived by the kindness of my mother who finished my pajamas. I loved my three years of Latin and the beautiful young woman who taught it. She was six feet tall and wore a pink and white cameo ring that seemed to me the most attractive I had seen. We respected each other, and I recall that she took me to Medina to see Greta Garbo in "Anna Karenina" when it opened in 1934. She pleased us all by sometimes playing the piano at lunchtime. My favorite was "Deep Purple," popular in 1938. She must have been a good teacher: My freshman year I was sent to a scholarship contest at Kent State College on the Latin I team.

I had a crush on the young male chemistry teacher but managed to have an explosion when demonstrating something about hydrogen and oxygen (could it have been water?) in front of an assembly. And I met and added another good friend to my list, Jane Crawford. She often came over, and we went horseback riding together. She had lived in California briefly and was the most interesting girl I knew. In our senior year we worked on the paper together, I as editor, she as business manager. Years later she married my cousin, Jim Beard, raised a son and a daughter, and taught school for many years.

One summer I went for two weeks to a camp near Wadsworth sponsored by the co-operative movement. It was an exhilarating experience. We had lectures and discussions on the co-op idea, ate a lot, played a lot, folk-danced a lot, sang a lot and above all flirted a lot. Everybody agreed it was wonderful.

The New York World's Fair opened in Queens, N.Y. in 1939. We didn't get to go to what sounded like unbelievably exciting displays; in fact, I never personally knew anyone who had enough money for that long trip. But some progress reached us: the weekly newsmagazine *Life* appeared in 1936 and was very big, and while I was in high school, Kleenex and Bird's Eye frozen vegetables came on the market.

It frequently happened during this time that I would have so much pain the first day of my menstrual period each month that I could not function for hours. I do not remember when or where or who the angel was who taught me the Knee Chest Position. It involved getting down on my knees in some private place, bending over until my shoulders touched the floor, keeping my back straight, and holding that position for as long as necessary. It did not take long. The pain would simply flow out of my body and I could function normally until the next month.

I was not good at team sports, never having been exposed to them. One year I was on the debating team, on the negative (in my opinion even then the wrong) side of the question of "Socialized Medicine" in the only debate I remember our team losing. I was editor of the newspaper my senior year and worked hard at it. I played a black maid in the senior play and worked hard at it, trying to acquire the Southern accent which I mistakenly assumed she would have. I did not have a boyfriend, though I sometimes had a date with a boy I did not much like or admire. I continued to enjoy the summers with Junior and to fantasize about George Richie. I had my first summer job, waiting tables at a restaurant in the park. I made decent tips~ because I tried hard and smiled a lot~but I hated the job.

An event occurred in 1935, when I was 16, that was to change my life. The Social Security Act was passed. As I write this, I have for 26 years now been a beneficiary of that Act, making my retirement years secure and free from worry. I fervently hope that my fellow citizens will never surrender this wonderful gift from FDR to the selfish interests that want to destroy it.

I was graduated in 1941 in a class of 19. Red being my favorite color, I chose a class ring with a ruby stone behind the seal; all the rest of the class chose gold. I left high school with five lifetime friendships. One of them was terminated by accidental death a few years ago, one ruined by Alzheimer's and then death, and one is in hiatus, Eileen having moved from her Florida apartment to a nursing home. Fern and I have been unable to find her despite strenuous efforts. Two are still active in our 91st year.

Because I learned to admire two of my high school teachers who had attended Muskingum College in New Concord, Ohio~halfway between Columbus and Pittsburgh~I ended up going there. It was then a Presbyterian school strongly dedicated to educating ministers and requiring every student to take courses in the Bible. In my day it gave its students little freedom to live adult lives. Many years later I learned it was often financially strapped and in danger of losing accreditation. Worst of all, it was an ivory tower. I did not learn about the dust bowl, the Okies and the thousands of families treking west to pick fruit for less than they needed to live on until, at 21, I saw the movie, *The Grapes of Wrath*.

Hitler was building a gigantic war machine in Germany, but we heard little of it. In fact, we still had a German exchange student on campus in the fall of 1939 when Poland was attacked. I had developed a friendship with the young woman. I really liked Helga (we never discussed politics) and felt guilty because Yadvega, my roommate that year, was from Poland, the country so shamefully attacked by Helga's. Little did we dream it was the first day of the all~encompassing struggle against fascism that would involve every one of us for years to come and drastically affect our lives!

We had an all~white faculty and student body and, on a campus of fewer than a thousand students~where everyone knew everyone~I never met a Jewish student or faculty member. In my sophomore year I started a campaign to admit black students and was immediately called into the office of the Dean of Women and threatened with expulsion. Only years later did I learn that I must have been there while John Glenn was. He was a "townie" who, I presume, majored in Science while I ended up with a major in Speech, one in Psychology and a minor in Physical Education. I should add that Muskingum College has in the past year or so become Muskingum University. I have no knowledge of it now. What I found to be shortcomings may have been cured.

I was in the honor society my freshman year. That year I had had a part-time job as a waitress in the dining room of the freshman dorm. The following summer I worked as a counselor at Camp He-Ya-Ta, the girls' camp of the Zanesville YWCA. In September, I was faced with not being able to return to Muskingum for lack of funds, but was offered a job working part-time with the Girl

3.1 Zanesville YWCA staff

Reserves, the Y's program for younger girls. From then on, my time and attention were divided, and I did not do honors work.

On one of my visits home, I learned that "Miss Dorothy," who had been the teacher in the "little room" when both Lu and I were there, had cancer. In those days, the word was never said, just intimated. My family and I went to visit her. She was married and had two little girls. Her home, which had been beautifully appointed, was a shambles, the costly wallpaper covered with crayon scribbles. Her husband, a friendly man who had conducted our very amateurish orchestra at church, was worn and worried, trying to keep up with the family and the farm. Not enough was known about her disease, and treatment was ineffective, if at all. She lay in her bed and bravely attempted to make conversation, but her suffering was clear. It was heartbreaking. We cannot but be grateful for the tremendous strides made in this field in the past 75 years.

I have mentioned living in the dorm my freshman year. I had a boyfriend that year, a Methodist minister's son appropriately named for John Wesley. He played trombone and would sometimes serenade me of an evening, standing in the valley and sending his love up to the dorm. This was romantic, but embarrassing, since the whole campus heard. It turned out I spent my sophomore year in the dorm, too, having been asked to be a counselor to the new freshmen. My reputation was somewhat sullied, however, by an elopement in which the girl descended from her room and met her lover just outside my first floor window. I was an extremely sound sleeper in those days and heard nothing! The housemother found that unbelievable.

There were no other dorms. One joined a club that had its own house. These were Greek letters but unconnected to national societies. I joined Chi Alpha Nu, called Kianu, with most of my friends but participated in few of its activities because of my frequent absences from the campus to work in Zanesville. One annual event I did enjoy was after we practiced for weeks, then all piled into a truck on a specified night and drove to each of the men's clubs in turn where we serenaded them.

My senior year, Yadviga, my Polish roommate our freshman year, finally felt enough at home on an American campus to apply to join Kianu. She was blackballed by a few members who claimed they would just not feel clean around her. This was to me a bolt from the blue. I had lived with her; she was so clean even God would have felt outdone. I protested but it was a *fait accompli* from which there seemed to be no recourse. The next year she was admitted.

My last three years I went out with Wes's roommate, Grant McClanahan, the son of a medical missionary, raised in Egypt and the most scholarly person I had known up to that time. He was studying Greek, already knew Arabic and had made some translations from it, was a fine tennis player and a writer, and hoped to become an archeologist. During the summer, while I was at home, he wrote and sent me a neat little hand-printed book called "Summer Thoughts." I have it still. It includes the poems "Spring Fever," "Note to Accompany a Corsage," "A Bio- and Psychological Appreciation of a Box of Candy Sent to Me as a Valentine" (I having been the fudge-maker and donor), and others, plus several essays including "Diognetus' Fable," "Arriving in Heaven" and "Bazaar Humor." I once quoted to him a verse of his, forgetting where I had read it:

"It grieves me that mankind has only two
Philosophies, which are the false and true.
The first rewards us not, the second is,
Alas, too difficult for me or you."
(Translated from the Arabic)

I attributed it to "some minor poet." He was amused and forgave me. I never failed to enjoy the time we spent together. It has come to my attention recently that he became a "distinguished career diplomat," who has written one book entitled *Diplomatic Immunity: Principles, Practices, Problems* (surely a bible for those following in his footsteps) and a second, *In an Ancient Land, a Memoir.*

In connection with my work for the YW, I attended a conference in Columbus where for the first time I heard a speaker who dealt with the rise of Hitler and Nazism. I was fascinated, stayed behind to ask him questions, and was disturbed that I was the only one who did.

The second experience occurred on campus. A black man had been engaged to come to speak to us. During the course of his talk, he told us that he had driven down from Columbus and there was no place on that long 75-mile drive where he could stop to use a restroom. I was shocked and outraged. At that point, my roommate was a working class kid from Cleveland, more savvy than most of the students. I suggested to her that we take him home and give him some food and a chance to rest before driving back. We did, to the curiosity of some of our sisters and the annoyance or consternation of others. He was a man of learning and charm and it turned out to be a pleasant visit. It left me with serious questions about our country's attitude toward its darker citizens.

Someone had established a small prize for Bible reading and a contest was held every year. I entered twice and won twice. The prize was $15, a respectable sum. My secret was picking passages that everyone loves.

As a freshman I had a three-pronged policy toward church-going: Once a month I went to the Methodist Church where Wes attended, once a month to the Presbyterian Church, where I never failed to be thrilled by the processional, "Ten Thousand Times Ten Thousand;" and two Sundays were reserved for washing hair, darning stockings (yes, we still did that; nylons had been invented but were prohibitively expensive), writing home and, if push came to shove, some studying. My religious fervor became less with each passing year but still motivated much of my thinking.

For three summers I was a counselor at He-Ya-Ta. I did whatever was required in the way of life-guarding and ran the dramatics program. At that point, I was familiar with some of the current plays on Broadway. I would tell the girls the story, we would pick a cast, and then each one would be encouraged and helped to work out her own dialogue. Some of our plays were quite good. If I had a girl who liked dramatics and had talent, that made all the difference. I loved that part of the work. Almost without exception, we hated the weekly day-long hikes across dusty roads in the heat of the day, with dry peanut butter sandwiches and water for lunch. Sun block had not been invented. The kids would arrive back at camp in various shades, some really burned. We would slather on Noxzema.

So that you will have a sense of the level of excitement at the camp, let me say that the two most dramatic events, aside from a really thrilling play we put on one year, were two bites I received–one from a snake and one from a horse–both the result of carelessness on my part, both startling and neither serious.

Since the pay was extremely modest, we seldom had a consistently high level staff. Our director, Miriam Koons, was an exception, but I remember one counselor, a teacher from Zanesville, so abysmally ignorant I couldn't understand how she got or held her job. The next summer, I persuaded my favorite psychology professor to join the staff, which brightened things up and temporarily raised the intellectual level. A visit by my sister one year for several weeks was a welcome lift for both campers and counselors. She was nicknamed "Sunny" and brought a cheerful attitude and endearing ways.

The end of college found me still not sure about a future career. Somehow I avoided becoming a teacher and tended to think I wanted to be a social worker. Having had three years of part-time experience with the Y, I expressed an interest in that direction and was invited to attend a 6-week National YWCA training program to be held at Oberlin College. It was an enjoyable experience, except for one sad —no, tragic—development. A sweet-faced young woman whose name I don't recall taught me to smoke. I didn't continue it immediately, but after going to work I began to find it relaxing to sit down in the late afternoon with a couple of staff people and have a smoke and a soft drink. Very soon I was hooked. For the next 40 years I struggled without success to break the habit. It was not until after I turned 65 and retired from full-time work--and with the help of Joan Daly and Marjorie Westfall, all of us trying to quit--that I succeeded. I am grateful every day for the 26 years I have been free of that insidious and dangerous habit. Near the end of the Oberlin course, I was offered a job in Charlotte, N.C. I had concluded that the South was where I wanted to be so I could learn as much about conditions as possible. I accepted the job at an annual salary of $1,500. At the end of the summer my parents drove me down, a lovely trip through the Blue Ridge Mountains.

What was the South like when I moved there in 1941? Total separation and segregation. Separate churches, separate schools, separate sections of town, separate restaurants, separate balconies in the movie theatres. Blacks in the back seats of the busses, whites in city hall. Demands by blacks for justice in the most outrageous situations but not yet for overall change. I found the segregation in the South shocking, but I had not traveled and did not know that many of the same conditions prevailed across the United States, even in New York City. Twelve years later I was in Washington, D.C. and had lunch with black friends on the very first day in 1953 when restaurants were allowed to serve everybody.

Looking back, I think the only qualification I had for my new job was enthusiasm. What I had to do was work with volunteer teachers in each school to form and conduct a club designed to put YWCA principles into practice. To organize, plan, inspire, follow through... that was it. I worked hard and did the best I could. I was far from an ideal Younger Girls' Secretary. My card files were in a shambles. Though I tried, I was not up on the latest dances the girls wanted to learn. I tended to be spontaneous, too willing to alter schedules when I was struck by a good idea. In competition with Girl Scout cookies, we sold potato chips, not exactly an inspiring substitute. My enthusiasm about improving black-white relations was off-putting to many, and I had additional shortcomings. But they put up with me for two years.

Among other duties, I was expected to chaperone dances for GI's. These were usually held on Saturday nights and involved no problems, often being fun. Jitterbugging was in but most of the dancing was to songs like "Where or When," "Deep Purple," "Now is the Hour," "White Cliffs of Dover" and "We'll Meet Again." But one Sunday afternoon I was at the Y while there were soldiers, who had come in from the large Army base outside of town, sitting around with nothing to do. They asked if they could dance, and I said, "Of course." The next day I learned there was general shock at my having allowed dancing on Sunday. It turned out to be a big No-No and my first introduction to the many differences between Northern and Southern mores and customs.

Another duty involved conducting devotions at meetings of the Board of Directors. When my name turned up on the schedule, I spent hours on my own time listening to Paul Robeson's *Ballad for Americans*, writing down the words, typing and mimeographing them so that the august board members would not miss one uplifting, inspiring and patriotic word of Paul's magnificent performance. I thought Paul and I had acquitted ourselves well, but after the meeting I was called into the director's office where I was told the Board wanted to fire me. I had scandalized them by playing a record by a "notorious communist." I was as innocent as a newborn babe about communism, so I protested and pointed out the American values involved in the *Ballad*. The director had integrity, good judgment and good sense. She knew I was telling the truth. I was not fired.

Living in the South was not easy for me. I learned to stay miles away from discussions of the Civil War, civil rights, and equal opportunities. But I was eager to learn. I called the local office of the NAACP, wanting information. Two impressive black gentlemen arrived to interview me. (I was unaware of it, but the building held its breath for the next hour.) My visitors turned out to be Kelly Alexander, head of the local organization, and Bishop Gordon of the AME Zionist Church. They were serious about wanting to know my motivations. I told them about my experience at college and my obvious need for information about conditions in Charlotte. The meeting ended amicably with their promise that they would be in touch with me. They were, having decided I was ignorant but honest. Along with a friend, Hannah Malkin, a case worker for the city and

3.2 NAACP Board

a native North Carolinian, I joined the NAACP and took part in its activities as long as I remained in town. We became good friends. They were courageous and resourceful people. The president of the local chapter, Kelly Alexander, later brought the North Carolina suit in the landmark case of <u>Brown v. Board of Education</u>, resulting in the end of *de jure*, though not *de facto*, segregation of school children in the U.S. Bishop Gordon was a dynamic, well-informed speaker, but forceful. I once invited one of the members of the YW board—the most enlightened—to attend a meeting at which he spoke. He was on fire and indeed inspiring but when it was over, my "liberal" friend said to me, "He makes me wonder why we freed them."

I sought and received cooperation from the black branch of the YW, operating out of a small house on a small budget but doing the same work I was attempting to do. We also became friends and developed a few programs together. I remember one that still makes my blood run cold, a large joint candlelight program in our building. It was a success as far as I could see but I resolved not to do it again: all those candles and all those girls with all that long hair!

On Sunday, December 7, 1941, Hannah and I attended the movie *Mrs. Miniver* in downtown Charlotte. This film is credited with doing much to rally support for Britain during WWII. It certainly had that effect on Hannah and me. When the appeal was made to help Britain in its defense against Hitler, both of us emptied our pockets. We walked out of the theatre into snow, very rare there, and, more importantly, newsboys on the streets with alarming news—Pearl Harbor attacked! We did not know where that was, but it sounded ominous. Having given all our cash, we had a long walk home in the falling snow with sober thoughts about what an unknown future would bring.

After Christmas I was invited to dinner by another young social worker. She and her two sisters had been entertaining soldiers from the local camp at the home they shared with their mother. One sister had gone back to college, leaving one soldier without a date. I was to be it. I wore my favorite dress—a bright red jersey. My date turned out to be named Clifford J. Hunter. All of us—soldiers and girls—ended up after dinner sitting on the floor having a good time sharing stories and jokes. For being so relaxed and informal, we were chided by the mother, but it was nevertheless a delightful evening. Cliff and I liked each other. He said he would call when he could get off the base.

Two weeks later I did receive a phone call from him. He had a pass and asked if I would have dinner with him. It was a rainy night, not a torrent but a steady drizzle. I was a little early and waited in happy anticipation. Cliff arrived a few minutes later in good spirits. I still remember the thrill when he came into the room. His raincoat was glistening and he seemed to bring in a hint of mist. He moved with such confidence, looked so handsome and appeared to be so pleased to be there that to this day I believe that in an instant I loved him. We were friends immediately, but it was not until the end of the meal that I knew I wanted to marry him.

He learned that I was one of two daughters of a rural mail carrier and a nurse, had grown up on a small farm in Ohio, and was a social worker at the local YW but not sure what I wanted to do the rest of my life. I learned that he was from Florida, was an art student, was sure he wanted to sculpt or paint the rest of his life, had been drafted into the Army and was awaiting a transfer to the Army Air Corps. I did not analyze his looks then, but thinking back, I know he was slender, of medium height, still a bit boyish looking, with blonde hair, lightly tanned skin, blue eyes, and an engaging smile.

From then on, we saw each other as often as he could get off the base. We spent time with some friends and had a few adventures that helped us know each other. On Easter Sunday we took a bus to visit friends. I had splurged on a handsome black suit and a white blouse. We were in good spirits. The bus became packed to the point of being overloaded. Cliff and I were sitting in the left hand seats

3.3 Cliff sculpting *Breadline*

just behind the driver. A black family got on, the woman carrying a tiny newborn baby. There was not an empty seat on the bus. We could not give our seats to the family, so I offered to hold the baby, and the mother handed it to me. Eventually they were able to move to the back of the bus and finally to find seats. She came back for the child. Jim Crow bus rules were bad for everyone~embarrassing, shameful, degrading and promoted ill feelings on both sides. The experience gave Cliff and me a chance to explore our feelings on race relations. He had worked with blacks one summer, all of them doing the same job in the watermelon fields of North Carolina. He recorded that experience in paint on canvas and it has hung on my wall for years.

Cliff was still awaiting transfer from the Army to the Army Air Corps. It developed this was going to take more time, and he was furloughed. He went to Crescent City to visit his parents, where he was able to resume painting though not the sculpture he would have preferred. He often wrote me and soon invited me to come for a visit. I arranged for time off and took the train to Florida. His family lived in a large Victorian house in town and owned a small orange grove nearby. His parents were welcoming and gracious. Both brothers were away in other branches of the service. We went swimming and boating and sightseeing, ate delicious sea food, and attended a seder (my first) at the home of Cliff's friends, the Kushners. We experimented with more caresses than we had in North Carolina and liked it. When the Army called him back, we traveled together on the train, chastely sitting up all night in a coach in spite of knowing that the train had one available bunk.

I learned on that trip that Cliff was not a good swimmer. In fact, for a boy who had grown up on a lake, he was a bad swimmer. I kidded him and later wished I had urged him to improve his performance in the water, though no amount of practice would have prepared him for the English Channel.

By this time, it was clear to each of us that we loved each other. As for all couples in wartime, the question was whether to marry now or wait. We finally decided to marry. Knowing Cliff would be called to the Air Corps any day, we picked a day a couple of weeks away, Saturday, June 6, 1942.

The wedding was set for the First Methodist Church, an imposing structure on Main Street. A friend volunteered to play the organ and someone found us a minister. I don't remember getting a license but we must have. I bought a tailored white silk suit and a hat, Cliff arranged for his best friend in the Army to be his best man, my sister came down from Chippewa to be my bridesmaid,

Wed To Air Officer

MRS. CLIFTON J. HUNTER

Mrs. Hunter, the former Miss Margaret Brown, daughter of Mr. and Mrs. Don M. Brown of Chippewa Lake, was married last Saturday to Lt. Clifton J. Hunter, son of Mrs. Alice Hunter of Crescent City, Fla. The ceremony was performed in the First Methodist church in Charlotte, N. C., where Mrs. Hunter is the Girl Reserve secretary for the Charlotte Y. W. C. A.

3.4 Maggie's wedding announcement in the Charlotte newspaper

the Hunters sent a gift of some family silver, the YWCA staff sent silver, the Board of Directors sent silver (the South was big on silver for weddings), and the president of the Board sent me an elegant real silk nightgown with real lace. Besides their daughter, my parents sent their congratulations, regrets at not being able to make the trip, and all their love and best wishes. The Y gave a breakfast for all the guests. We even had a 4-day honeymoon in the Carolina mountains, from whence I returned with poison ivy. I soon saw a doctor who gave me a shot and I was never again troubled by that scourge. But no pregnancy. Before the wedding Cliff had gone with me to my doctor where I was fitted for a diaphragm.

During the next month, I was tied up at the Y camp outside of Charlotte, and he was tied up at the Army camp. We saw each other once or twice. Then he had to go. It was heartbreaking to be separated so soon. We wrote a lot. I worried that he would soon be learning to fly and might crash. I decided the best plan for me was also to learn to fly, then I could stop worrying. There was a small airport a few miles from town where I enrolled for lessons costing $6 an hour. I also signed up for courses in meteorology and navigation.

Learning to fly a Piper Cub was a piece of cake compared to what Cliff was undergoing in California, so when he wrote he was having trouble soloing, I told my instructor, and in a brief time he let me go up alone. I wired Cliff, "Soloed today, darling." He took the wire to his instructor, who decided he was ready and allowed him to solo.

I found I had one other worry. In our haste to wed, we had not had time to learn if we really were the same kind of people. I stopped worrying when I received the following letter:

My Adorable, Progressive, Air-minded Wife:

The NAACP meeting must have been exciting. It's the sort of thing I got such a kick out of in N.Y., though they were usually "commies" and liberals and CCNY students fighting Mayor Hague, or protesting against our policy toward Loyalist Spain during their struggle, etc. But it's the same thing, isn't it? A small group of progressives, knowing the odds against them, but fighting anyhow, gaining ground inch by inch. Makes you appreciate our democracy to realize such meetings aren't going to be busted up by S.S. and also to realize its great failings that such meetings are necessary. Too bad such a pitiful small number of the people know or care what is going on under their noses. Would like very much to have been there with you. I haven't been up in the air over a cause for so long (there's opportunity for a pun, but I won't make it) that I'm beginning to look like a Republican.

Cliff was an enthusiastic bridge player. When he came down with a fever and sore throat and was confined to the base hospital for the first time since being drafted, he found three other bridge players, and they had a spirited daily game, to their intense pleasure. Day after day, Cliff's temperature stayed up, especially the reading taken late in the afternoon, only to return to normal one day when there was no game. Bridge fever had kept him on the sick list for three or four days!

I found the flying lessons eating into both my limited time and even more limited money, so I took a few more, decided I was no fledgling Earhart and quit. As to the courses, one was too hard for me, and the other too boring. Maybe still adorable, certainly still progressive, but no longer very air-minded.

Meanwhile in Charlotte, my life was busy. I had decided younger girls were not my cup of tea, but I thought I would enjoy working with older, serious-minded young women employed in shops and factories. I resolved that when the chance came I would seek more training and prepare for such a change. Hannah had become my best friend and was changing the way I looked at society, opening up avenues unknown to me, giving me an elementary introduction to the labor movement and Marxism, Through our work with the NAACP, I was becoming more familiar with the race relations questions that bothered and interested me and developing friendships with some of the people we worked with, including a couple on the faculty at Johnson C. Smith University.

Finally, in the Spring, Cliff became a Second Lieutenant and could invite me to join him. I received a letter from Stockton, California, saying:

Sugar, if you're here around the middle of April, I'll welcome you with open arms... We just breezed through the town in the wee hours of the morning, so I don't know what sort of place it is... But we'll be together again, honey, all that matters to me, and I won't be living in bachelor officers' quarters. It'll be our little love nest (or probably somebody's back room or hay loft, depending on the housing situation).

I gave notice on my job, packed, closed up shop, booked a ticket to Stockton and said goodbye to my friends and Charlotte.

IV
CALIFORNIA, NEW MEXICO, ARIZONA & NEBRASKA (1943-1944)

The 5-day train ride from Charlotte to Stockton was a nightmare but I was so buoyed up I took it in stride. Upon leaving Charlotte, I found I had no seat. This was in contrast to my trip before the war.

Then I was five minutes late and they held the train for me. Though I was a nobody, I had a reservation. In 1943 I spent the night with dozens of others sitting on the floor in the aisle, those needing to pass stepping over us. Somewhere down the road, probably past Washington,

4.1 Cliff as pilot in US Army Air Force

things eased and there were a few seats. The crowding, the jostling, the stopped-up toilets continued across the country. It got worse at Salt Lake City when the air conditioning broke down. All the windows were flung open and from then on we were covered with soot and dust. Only the glory of California, when we reached it, made the last day bearable. When we finally arrived in Stockton, I got a room at the Y and spent hours showering, soaking and scrubbing. I had never been so dirty. The dress I was wearing was so filthy I discarded it. I was reasonably tidy, though terribly tired, when Cliff finally found me.

I rented a room with a widow lady whose greatest joy in life seemed to be her glass of beer and game of solitaire every evening. Cliff was able to visit me only infrequently but knowing there was no longer a continent between us made me content. We were not there long.

The next stop was Sacramento, where I rented an apartment for $65 a month so elegant I felt like Mrs. Rockefeller. I liked the city, with its east-west streets named for the alphabet and its north-south streets numbered. But I had nothing to do. The first (probably the only) interracial USO was located there. I volunteered to do its office work, socialize with the soldiers who came to visit, and whatever else I could that would be useful. The director was a gentle and dedicated man, a member of the Baha'i religion, believing in the spiritual unity of mankind.

The months flew by, bringing us to Hobbs, New Mexico. These transfers were made by car, traveling at top speed to try to find housing for the wives before the whole contingent arrived. Hobbs turned out to be an oil town and smelled like it. What little I saw of it was flat and ugly. I got a room at a motel where there were several other wives we knew. We sometimes exercised together and on occasion fixed joint breakfasts for the men before they took off at daybreak.

I wanted to pick cotton. The country's need was great and I was willing to attempt the heat, fatigue and sore fingers. Cliff disappointed me, taking a stuffy attitude that it would not be fitting for an officer's wife. It was perhaps the only time we disagreed.

Next stop, Tucson. I had a room with a friendly family. While there, I was invited to travel with one of the wives to Texas to visit her husband's family at their cattle ranch. For a few days we lived high on the hog. I remember yellow-meated watermelons cooled in a deep well. On the way back I saw the famous King ranch and marveled that some could have so much wealth and others so little. That trip occurred in the middle of summer in Texas, in a car without an air conditioner, memorable for that reason if no other.

Cliff was then transferred to Alamogordo, New Mexico, near the White Sands. I could not find lodging for love or money so I got a job as a mother's helper in a doctor's home, where I proceeded to scorch more dainty little dresses for a three-year-old than you would believe. I had one interesting experience, the doctor inviting me to accompany him while he delivered a baby to a Mexican American woman whose husband was in service. It was a girl and a great disappointment to the mother, who cried bitterly because her husband wanted a boy. The doctor told me she would be over that by the next day and happy with her baby.

Being able to visit such parts of the White Sands as were not preempted by the Proving Grounds was a never-to-be-forgotten treat. Everything really is white, even the animals.

From there we were sent to Lincoln, Nebraska, the jumping off point. Our stay was brief. Cliff was excited about finally getting into action. I was sad but trying to make the best of it. That was the last time I saw him.

ENTR'ACTE
DAD, MOM AND LU

DAD

Don M. Brown, my father, had natural intelligence and spent his life learning. He was a good listener, always eager for knowledge. He seemed to have an unlimited capacity for work, but he was also always ready for fun, whether it was going to the beach on summer evenings when work and chores were done, or taking a walk with Mom, or playing Monopoly or rummy or chess. He was one of four children, having two older brothers, Dale and Lloyd, and a twin sister, Dorothy.

E 1.1 The Browns with Sharon

Dad constantly worked to make life better, bringing electricity to the town, learning to build a barn, piping spring water into our house and barn, learning to plant and care for an orchard, learning to raise bees, learning to run a dairy~and all the time working a long and tiring day delivering the mail across country roads, many of them unpaved, often in a Model T held together with wire from a nearby fence. When the weather was really bad, he rode on horseback, perhaps with a tire someone had ordered from Sears, Roebuck around the horse's neck.

Always open to new ideas and ready to learn, Dad spent many winter evenings studying seed catalogues in preparation for the coming planting season. But he did more. In the 1930's he began to read about revolutionary ideas of raising crops without chemicals~the organic way~and adopted those methods whenever he could.

With Mom's full cooperation, he went to law school in Akron,

20 miles away, three nights a week after work for three years, a back-breaking schedule superimposed on his work, the farm, a business and, part of the time, caring for an invalid wife. The irony was that just before his graduation, the state changed the law so that any person not having the bachelor's degree could not take the bar exam. Dad became a Justice of the Peace and judiciously advised the patrons along his route *gratis*.

Dad took part in all our family plans, picnics, and holidays. He was a member of the volunteer fire department and worked in programs to benefit veterans and special events run by the church, including amateur theatricals. And when it became apparent serious efforts would be needed to expand the local school system to include high school, he became president of the Board of Education. He was almost always cheerful and hopeful, always affectionate, seldom angry, never violent, and never profane. The worst thing I ever heard him say was "gol darn the luck!"

When he retired after 25 years, he and Mom sub-divided our farm into lots and built well-designed and well-constructed brick houses, one at a time, doing all the work themselves except for excavation of the basements and erection of the chimneys. If a house did not sell within a reasonable time, they would furnish it and move in. It worked like a charm. The house sold in short order. Dad also became a real estate agent, selling farms he knew from years of driving past and observing them. During this period, he became blind from cataracts, it then being the policy to let this occur before scheduling an operation. Mom rose to the occasion, driving him to appointments, doing the paper work, even becoming a registered real estate agent herself, until his sight was restored.

Mom had always dreamed of going back to Morgan County. She and Dad for many years owned a tract of land there and our family from time to time would visit to plant trees or tend them, my parents believing in reforestation. They finally bought a mellow old brick house on the Muskingum River and lived there summers, raising and preserving their food, and every autumn driving to Tucson where they owned a small house in a senior development outside of town. They were able to do this for several years and found it a happy way to live. They celebrated their 50th anniversary in Arizona and Dad found new hobbies there. In his 70's, besides taking up a little golf, he started working on the potter's wheel and made a whole series of pieces, each one better than the one before. I cherish a pitcher, a casserole and a bowl that I own.

Dad died too soon, only 74, but it was the kind of death one dreams of. Taking his morning walk in the desert, doing his exercises in the living room one minute, dead of a cerebral hemorrhage the next, before Mom could cross the room. He was a Mason and was duly buried in the traditional apron.

For 80 years one question has puzzled me. Why was my father, a loving and generous man, a bigot? The only answer I can find is that in his whole lifetime, he never met or got to know any black people. He was raised in the country, near Swanton, where there were no blacks; he was drafted into a segregated Army, and then moved to Chippewa, where, as we have seen, the only black family lasted but briefly and he never knew them. This does not excuse his actions but it does help explain them.

MOM

Mom, on the other hand, was not bigoted. As a young woman she had had a chance to live and work in the South where she met and got to know black people. She always had a wonderful way of accepting everybody she met. She might not approve of them, but she was able immediately to know where they were coming from and appreciate them as equal human beings.

My mother, Peggy Brown, had a great capacity to love. She especially loved her family and friends, with an almost fierce loyalty. She was small but strong and tireless. All her life she worked hard, moving with quick steps on her tiny feet from task to task to help others. She had grit and determination to keep going in spite of many bouts with ill health and at the end excruciating pain. She was devoted to her four brothers, Jesse Charles, called "Jay," George Raymond, called "Bill," Charles Frederick, called "Abe," and "Fred," whose real name

I don't remember but I'll bet anything it wasn't Frederick. Mom was also devoted to one half-sister, Villa, a daughter of her mother's first marriage, and just as opposed to another, Garnet, a daughter of her father's first, finding her values false.

Mom had a brilliant mind and an extraordinary memory. She loved history and she loved poetry, both reading and writing it. She was dedicated to learning and struggled not only for her own education as a teacher and then a nurse but to help Donnie, as she always called him, attend law school and to send her daughters to college in a day when many still felt that educating girls was a waste of money. And she retained what she had learned. I remember Dad coming into the house to consult her one day. He was building our barn and needed help. Mom worked out the geometry for him.

She was versatile, knowing how to do almost everything and quick to learn what she didn't know. Our house and clothes were always clean. She did the ironing in an hour on a machine called a mangle. She made our butter and cottage cheese. She knew how to grow everything, cook everything, can everything, preserve everything, freeze everything, bake everything—except bread, which she simply refused to make and we had to buy. She could sew, making all our clothes when we were small. And she always raised a garden, both vegetables and flowers.

She was a great conversationalist, able to talk interestingly and get others to respond. She was also a fine story-teller. We often lingered long at the dinner table to hear her tell a tale.

Mom always insisted on some income of her own. She raised chickens, selling the young roosters as broilers and keeping the hens for their eggs. She made huge quantities of apple butter every fall in a great iron kettle in the backyard, to be gifted or sold. And having earned the money, she had an unbelievable capacity to hold on to it. I never remember an emergency when Mom did not come up with money, small in amount but equal to the need.

She loved the outdoors, taking daily walks to see the sun rise or set. Dad often joined her in the evenings. They always returned looking more serene. She also loved animals, especially little orphans. From time to time, the creek behind our house would flood and tiny little

Mallard ducklings would be found when the waters receded. Mom would adopt them and mother them as long as they lived.

Mom joined the Eastern Star, a fraternal organization open to women related to Masons. She became Ruth, the Biblical character who gleaned in the fields to provide for herself and her aged mother-in-law. Lu and I used to giggle as we stood at the top of the basement stairs and heard her declaiming her lines over the chugging of the washing machine.

Mom always believed that somewhere in her family tree there was a great-great-great grandfather Green, who had fought in the American Revolution. Was this Nathanael Green, the Quaker and smith who started as a private and ended as one of Washington's most trusted officers?

And finally, Mom took pride in her profession. Doctors with very ill patients sometimes pleaded with her to take the case because the care she gave was always beyond the call of duty. She extended the same concern to neighbors when they needed her. And this quality was with her all her life. In the days before Medicare made crutches and wheelchairs available, Mom tried to set up a fund in the senior housing center in Tucson where they lived to supply people of limited income and physical problems with such therapeutic aids.

Most of all, Mom never abandoned me. She could not change Dad's mind but she could give me a gift and rejoice with me over Mindy's birth. I think she found having a namesake vastly pleasing; it was my heartfelt tribute to her. She tried to keep the lines of communication open between us, writing me frequently, once sending the police to locate me when I delayed answering, and always welcoming me when I went to visit. She loved me with a colossal love. I always knew it and too often took her for granted.

MY SISTER LU

My only sibling, Lucile Idele Brown Reiser, was born in our farmhouse in Chippewa Lake on a hot August day in 1922. Our mother weighed 98 pounds and the baby 13, so that even though there was a doctor in attendance, the birth lasted two days and nights, and resulted in a broken jaw for Lu, a mother so grievously injured she could have no more children, and a household so exhausted no one could remember when Lu had actually arrived. They picked August 30.

Lu was always pretty~even beautiful~throughout her life. In spite of her arduous beginning, by three she was a healthy, dimpled, blue~eyed blonde with abundant wavy hair, a love of people, and an engaging disposition. Then she suffered the series of childhood

E 1.2 Lu

diseases and broken bones previously related, but she came back a fighter. She played a deadly game of Monopoly, never giving up until she won. She was my defender. Bullying is much in the news now in 2011, but it was not unknown almost a century earlier. One day we were walking home from school when some older kids started making fun of me: I was the only kid who wore glasses, I liked school, and I got good grades. I was saying nothing to defend myself. Suddenly Lu, half their size, ran at them, swinging her metal lunch box furiously, intending not just to scare but to hurt them. But she could be as loving and sympathetic as she was fierce. When I became a camp counselor years later, she became a junior counselor. Overnight she was the most popular person in camp and was nicknamed "Sunny" for her happy temperament.

As we grew up, I found myself without any particular direction. Lu always knew she wanted to follow in Mom's footsteps and become a nurse. She entered a 4-year program for a B.S. and an R.N., completed the required year of college and entered her hospital training, so determined to get her cap (to be bestowed after six weeks) that she kept going in spite of a severe cold. The cold became full-blown walking pneumonia and she was given large doses of a new miracle drug–sulfa. The treatment destroyed enough red blood corpuscles that for the next year she was unable to walk up stairs. She went home and was nursed back to health, but by then the tuition money was gone. She took a business course and got a job.

In June of 1942 she came to North Carolina to be my bridesmaid and met a sailor at a dance. He told her he was from Toledo and she told him she was from Cleveland. Then he added, "Not really Toledo, Napoleon" and she confessed "Not really Cleveland, Chippewa Lake." Based on his being a good dancer, a physical therapist and handsome and her being charming, beautiful and hoping for a career in medicine, it was inevitable that they lose no time in contemplating a life together. I was her matron of honor in September when she married James Reiser, a marriage that lasted over 50 years until his death.

Shortly after the end of World War II, they moved to Tucson, Arizona, where Jim planned to pick up the practice he had before going into the Navy. They had a daughter named Sharon and then a son named Don. Lu's greatest love when she was small had been dolls and babies; there was never any question that she would be an outstanding mother. She was also a good wife, in full partnership with Jim. They worked hard and did well. Starting in a tiny house, they moved up. Every few years there would be a new home until finally they owned a large property on a mountain overlooking the city. It was a magnificent adobe, beautifully furnished with American Indian artifacts and western style furniture. It came complete with peacocks! The Reisers lived there happily for 17 years; peacocks do not take to moving and are probably still there.

In 1963, Lu resumed her efforts to become a nurse. Being then over 35, she was not permitted under Arizona law to become an R.N., but she was able to complete an L.P.N. degree and got a job with the County working with a Baby Keep Well program. She was in seventh heaven. Meanwhile, Mom and Dad were spending winters in Tucson, returning to Ohio for the summers. But in 1971, Dad suddenly died of a cerebral hemorrhage. Mom lived alone in Tucson until she fell and broke a hip, thereafter needing someone to oversee her care. It necessarily fell to Lu's lot. To have dreamed so long, worked so hard, and finally achieved her goal-and then to have to give it up-was a most bitter pill.

After the death of both parents, Lu did a gracious and loving act. She and Jim came to visit me in New Jersey, ending the long and painful separation imposed on my family by my father. When Jim was diagnosed with cancer, Lu with the help of a hospice lovingly oversaw his care until his death. Well into her 80's, she developed stomach cancer that metastasized into lung cancer-a heavy sentence for a woman who had never smoked. She had moved to Oregon to be near Sharon, who was practicing medicine in Roseburg. Don, wanting to be near enough to take care of his mother and looking for a career change, had moved with her. Surrounded by her children and grandchildren, Lu bore her long and devastating illness with grace, dying on March 29, 2009.

V
NEW JERSEY
(1945-1953)

As soon as Cliff left Lincoln, I headed for Ohio and home. My parents and Lu, who was living with them while Jim was stationed on Trinidad with the Navy, were glad to welcome me. After a brief period of worry, I learned that Cliff had successfully flown his B26 to England and was in a camp there. But I

5.1 Lu with Maggie at Willowdale

soon became restless. Too many new ideas were in my head, and I wanted to give them a try. By then, Hannah had settled in New York City, sharing an apartment on Central Park West with her sister. In 1944 she invited me for a visit. As the train drew into the city, I was bursting with anticipation. After a happy visit, I settled down.

I went to Columbia University to explore the possibility of getting an MSW and was confronted with so many requirements that I gave up. I knew the progressive movement had just opened the Jefferson School. I went down to see them. They were still sweeping up the plaster and I enrolled in a course or two, notably one in philosophy.

Paul Robeson was appearing in Othello with Jose Ferrer as Iago and Uta Hagen as Desdemona. Hannah and I went to see them. Hannah, who is a good deal more earthy than I, remarked when it was over, "There wasn't a dry seat among all the women in the house." The play was widely acknowledged to be "one of the most memorable events in the history of the theatre." It broke all records for Shakespearean productions on Broadway, with a record run of 296 consecutive performances.

Remembering Cliff's friendship with Meyer Kushner, I decided to seek out the family. Cliff had known the elder Kushners in Crescent City. As a teenager he had helped out in their store. When his father's orange crop failed and Cliff had to drop out of college, they arranged with their nephews in New Jersey~house and sign painters~to give Cliff a job and a place to live so he could continue his art education. I had in my possession a letter from Meyer to Cliff which said:

> I have always been thinking of you. I kind of took a liking
> to you since the first time I talked to you. You sort of
> symbolized America to me.

I called Meyer, went to see him and his wife, Shane, and was utterly captivated. They found a room for me next door and I moved to West New York, N.J. a few days later. I continued to attend my classes at the Jefferson School. In the course of one philosophy lecture, I was converted to atheism. For the first time in my life, I felt free from fear. It was the most exhilarating experience of my life. Riding back to New Jersey that night on the bus, I felt I could weep, I could sing, I could fly.

I was to need all that strength. A few evenings later I received a telegram from the War Department saying that Cliff was missing in action. I went back to New York, got on the subway and rode all night. I couldn't cry, I couldn't think coherently. All I could do was hold on to hope. I resolved to visit the Hunters in Florida and did, a sadly different time from the first. For an age we waited for news. I had no way of contacting the families of the other crew members. They had been was assembled just before departure and I never met them.

Late in April I received from Cliff's brother Phillips a copy of a letter he had received from the executive officer of the 577th Bombardment Squadron. It said:

> [I]n regard to your brother the facts are as follows: his
> flight was on a mission into France. On completing

their "bomb run" on the target, it set course for home base in England. Your brother's ship evidently was hit by flak and developed motor trouble. As the flight started back across the Channel, his ship lagged behind the formation with three motors feathered. With the altitude he had, he evidently tried to make it across and to safety. Unfortunately, he had to crash land in the Channel, only a few miles from the English coast, and your brother got out of the ship all right and to safety momentarily, then he returned to help a crew member in distress. He was drowned in this act of heroism, being unable to reach the dinghy from which survivors were rescued. He gave his life in an effort to save one of his crew men.[1]

As soon as hope was gone, I really started to mourn. I cried so hard and so much that I have never again been able to cry at the loss of any other person—not my mother and father, not my second husband, not my boss of 42 years, not my dearest friends.

June 6, 1944, the second anniversary of our wedding, brought no joy for that reason, just a sharper pain personally, but that date was also D-Day when hundreds of thousands of our troops stormed and invaded France to bring the war to Hitler's own backyard. D-Day brought hope to millions that the terrible suffering around the world would someday soon end. I now know that many of our hopes were simply dreams.[2]

I began to realize that in spite of my grief, if I wanted to eat I would have to find a job. Wanting to help with the war effort, I went down to a factory in Union City I knew was an organized shop. It was not hiring, but I learned that the local union (I believe 448) needed a secretary. I had had half a year of typing in high school. I figured I could do the job, applied and was hired. The business agent began to educate me on labor history, especially the history of the Congress of Industrial Organizations (CIO) and the United Electrical, Radio & Machine Workers of America (UE), affiliated with it.

Meanwhile, I was remembering what I had leaned from Hannah

1   The War Department wrote me on July 16, 1944 confirming that Cliff had died on March 5 while returning from a bombardment mission to Merignac, France.

2   See Chapter 16, "A People's War?" in Howard Zinn's "A Peoples History of the United States.."

and hoping to learn more. I looked for the progressive movement and found some folks. I began to attend sessions to expand my extremely limited knowledge of politics. But I was very sad. The Army Air Corp sponsored a meeting of the widows and other dependents of flyers who had been lost. It was held in Weequahic Park, Newark. I did not know how to get there by bus so had to hire a cab, a costly undertaking. About a dozen people attended, mostly widows. There was a ceremony and a photo was taken and later sent to us. It was 8-1/2 x 11 and in color. Everybody looked reasonably happy and in control except me. I looked so sad that I could not bear to keep the picture around and destroyed it. About this time my mother and sister came to visit and found me still inconsolable. I was eventually rescued by a couple who invited me to leave the lonely room where I was living and share their apartment in Jersey City.

In the meantime, Roosevelt had signed orders putting the Japanese Americans in detention camps for the duration, and the situation regarding blacks could be summed up this way:

> The Army jim-crows us. The Navy lets us serve only as
> messmen. The Red Cross refuses our blood. Employers
> and labor unions shut us out. Lynchings continue. We are
> disenfranchised, jim-crowed, spat upon.

My job at Local 448 was the beginning of my new "career." After that I was to work at the Bayonne Local, Jersey City Local 427, and UE District 4 in Newark.

Once, during those years, I did something I had never done before nor since. I had been thinking about the role of women in the labor movement, realizing how negligible their role was and how much potential strength could be added to labor's fight if they had a chance to participate fully. I may have made a nuisance of myself by pressing these issues, but I was given a chance to make a speech at a convention of the Hudson County CIO. There was a large gathering. I had worked out an inspired speech, wore a bright red linen dress, delivered my remarks with gusto and received a good hand and that was the end of that. Time and the feminist movement were needed. Betty Friedan's book *The Feminine Mystique* did not come out until 1963.

Later I began to hear about a union man who had walked the

picketline in the snow, day after day, cardboard lining the holes in his shoes, during a long, badly-timed strike against the American Radiator Company. His name was Ernie Thompson. He was black and he was Secretary of the Hudson County CIO Council, overwhelmingly made up of white members.

5.2 Ernie when we met

I hoped to meet him some day and finally attended a meeting where he was present. As I walked by, I noticed him looking at my legs, which were then tanned and shapely. When the meeting ended, I had a chance to see that he was tall, erect, strongly muscled, having a medium brown complexion, beautiful brown eyes and a pleasant expression--friendly when he smiled or laughed. I knew he had a nice voice, could talk convincingly, and his opinions were much respected. Time went by. I learned that the day after Pearl Harbor he had visited all four recruiting stations, desperately trying, without success, to join the Army, the Navy, the Air Force, or the Coast Guard. He was blind in one eye, the midwife who attended his birth having used the wrong drops. It was not noticeable and never seemed to cause him any difficulty.

Another meeting occurred, at the end of which (it was a Saturday night) I found myself with nothing to do. I learned that Ernie was going to Harlem. I had heard a lot about it but had never been there. It turned out he was going alone and I asked if I could go along. He had listened to my speech at the convention and had observed me at meetings. He said yes, and we walked to the train. It was crowded, and we became separated, but he managed to find a seat on the other side of the aisle. I saw him sit down and also saw there was a vacant seat beside him. I hesitated. I knew if I took that seat I had better mean it, that it was a commitment to a new way of life. I crossed the aisle through the crowd and took the seat.

Ernie knew Harlem like the back of his hand. We went to Small's

Paradise, the popular dance place. It was crowded, but we found seats with a group of four or five others out for the evening. They were not hostile to me; in fact they were friendly.

Ernie and I danced a few times. We had a drink. We talked. We started to kiss in the most natural and friendly fashion. We left there and went to another famous watering hole. We walked all around Sugar Hill. Morning started to break, and we found a breakfast joint where we had bacon and eggs. It was time to go home. We got off the train and started walking down an alley where we stopped to kiss some more. We suddenly heard footsteps behind us and guiltily broke away, both of us suddenly aware we were back in Jersey and real life.

It does not take me long to make up my mind when I find what I am looking for. Ernie was what I was looking for, and he was of the same mind. At the union office in Bayonne where I worked there were long flights of steps up to the bathroom. I found myself so joyful that I always took them two steps at a time, and this refrain kept running through my head, "I love him and I'm going to marry him."

Ernie was just then assigned to a Campbell's Soup factory on the Eastern Shore of Maryland where there was a strike. He wrote me: "I find it hard to put my feelings into words, so powerful is my love for you. You have possessed my thoughts and my being so completely, I am not growing weak, but strong and sure-working with a song in my soul for the first time in ages."

But much as we were in love, there were problems. He was in the process of divorce, his wife, fed up with unions and strikes and unemployment, had several years before, without notice to him, moved herself out, with the two children and all the furniture. Ernie had filed for divorce but Hudson County was then a Catholic county where divorces were often stalled for years.

We continued to date, sometimes breaking up but never able to stay apart. One of the most satisfactory dates we had involved driving to a quiet spot where we somehow started talking about our religious experiences as children. We had both been raised in the Methodist Church and agreed that its hymns were better than those of any other denomination. For the next two hours we took turns recalling our favorites and singing them. Both of us knew and could sing an amazing number. It was wonderful fun. We never did it again.

Another date stays in my memory. We had spent the night in a hotel in Harlem, a rare treat we could seldom afford. The next morning we started to return to New Jersey by conventional means but decided instead to walk the length of Central Park. It may not be one of the Seven Wonders of the World either on the ancient or the new list, but it is a magical experience to visit it up close. We walked and looked and lingered for several hours.

Ernie was a sensitive and caring sexual partner. We had been together for a few months, and I was still having trouble having an orgasm. One night, parked in his old car, usually our only refuge for tender moments, he said, "Don't worry, we'll get some help for you." Such concern and kindness was all I needed. Within five minutes I had success. To borrow a word from Louis Armstrong, fantastic! fantastic! fantastic!

By 1945 we were beginning to be hopeful that the war, at least in Europe, would soon be over. Then lightning struck. FDR on April 12th suffered a cerebral hemorrhage and died. We were like children who have lost their father. This was our leader, who had cheered us on to fight for freedom of speech and worship, freedom against want and fear, in the face of the worst regime the world had yet seen. Everything stopped. My friends and I met and were comforted by being reminded that Roosevelt was a great man because he possessed qualities which made him capable of serving the great social needs of his time, but that only the people are immortal. The forces for progress that were in motion would continue and peace would come. But a voice the world needed had been stilled.

In March of 1946, Winston Churchill made his "Iron Curtain" speech in Missouri, marking the beginning of the Cold War. All too soon we learned those relatively halcyon days under Roosevelt were gone. President Truman, who had twice dropped atomic bombs on Japan, and proceeded to throw out the New Deal programs and create the Cold War, endorsing Churchill's philosophy. Growing out of that was the Korean War and the Senator Joe McCarthy anti-Communist period.

By 1947, both Ernie and I were working in Local 427, Jersey City.

Downstairs from our office in the National Newark & Essex Bank Building there was a small branch of Brooks Brothers that also carried some women's fashions. It was the time of the "New Look." I found I was still a perfect 12 and looked so good in the new longer styles after the short skimpy clothes of wartime, I could not resist. When things went on sale, I stretched the budget thin and bought a smart looking spring coat, a skirt and a top or two. Later, when Christmas approached, I went back and found a suit and an overcoat in Ernie's size, at prices I could afford. I joyfully presented them to him. He looked wonderful in them but to my great disappointment made me take them back, saying he appreciated the thought but could make do without the clothes. I recalled this incident at Christmas in 2010 when I found a beautiful shirt and tie at a ridiculous price and asked Josh if he would accept them. He said exactly what his father had said when Josh was nine years old:.He appreciated the offer but could make do without the clothes.

On April 15 of 1947, an event occurred which raised the hearts and hopes of many in the country and most especially the black people. Branch Rickey hired Jackie Robinson to be a member of the Brooklyn Dodgers, for the first time breaking the color line in baseball. Robinson endured inhuman mistreatment by other players and fans but finished his first year as National Rookie of the Year. Ernie was a baseball fan; I was not but became and remained one until the sad day when the team left Brooklyn. Robinson's total career was so outstanding that his number 42 is forever retired from baseball and will never be used again once the only player currently wearing it retires.

One of my tasks at 427 was helping to handle the Mario Russo Memorial Fund. Russo was a young member of the Phelps Dodge local during a bitter and historic strike. The company sent armed goons to break it up and Russo was killed. He left a wife and four small children. District 4 raised $20,000, quite a princely sum in those days, to help the family. Mort was the trustee; I did the bookkeeping and over the 20 years accounted for all but three cents.

In the meantime, Ernie had an idea. He would arrange with his friend Paul Robeson for a concert sponsored by the union. Paul agreed and a fee was set. Efforts were made to sell the tickets, but few of the members had heard of Robeson and did not realize what a treat it was to hear him. Paul was still young, in good voice, and as always generous in presenting a full, exciting program. It was a great concert, but attendance was small. At the end, Ernie had to meet with Paul and tell him the gate was not large enough for his fee. Paul did not hesitate. He said, "You have enough for my accompanist and for the hall. I'll take whatever is left."

Ernie and I continued to work together and to date but ran into every possible opposition, including from the most enlightened and advanced people we knew, Joe Fischer among them. I moved to the home of a young couple and later to a $7 a week room with a stranger, a black woman who did not approve but had a certain fairness about her. I finally decided to buy a house and found one on Forrest Street in Jersey City near Jackson Avenue. It was a 4-story brick house that had been subdivided into an apartment on each floor. There were no vacant apartments, but I bought it anyway, figuring something would open up. The price was $2,000. I had to borrow from the real estate agent his commission of $250 to get through the closing.

Then began months of making the place less drab and more inviting. Both Ernie and I spent many hours cleaning and painting. One apartment became vacant and I invited Joe Squires, another UE organizer, and his wife Bobby to share it with me. Joe was a friend of Ernie's and had been a construction worker in his hometown of St. Louis. He pitched in. But I still had no apartment of my own. A gambler occupied the top floor. I hired a New York detective who got the goods on him, and after several weeks he moved out, and I was eventually able to move in.

In 1948 an elderly white junk dealer was killed in Trenton, N.J. Six young black men were arrested, and five of them confessed. Oddly enough, the motive was supposed to be robbery, yet $1,500 was found on the person of the dead man. An all-white jury nevertheless sentenced all six to die. The case is often compared to that of the Scottsboro Boys. The Civil Rights Congress, of which I was a member, was led in New Jersey by a courageous man named Lewis Moroze. It took up the case and wider support came from the NAACP and the

ACLU. One of the lawyers on the case was Emanuel Bloch, later to be the attorney for the Rosenbergs. The Six were retried in 1951 and four of them acquitted. In 1952, the other two were retried, but one of them died of a heart attack and the sixth was set free for time served.

When people no longer have leadership urging them to think hopeful, forward-looking thoughts, they turn to small, petty thoughts. Thus, personal trouble turned up for Ernie and me. There began to be talk about our dating. It eventually affected the leadership, and I was fired. Here I was with a mortgage, a house, tenants, debts for the refrigerator and other equipment I had bought for my own apartment, and no income except the $50 a month which the Army insurance policy paid. I went home to Chippewa. My sister was then about to give birth to her first child. The family had learned that there was a problem with negative blood which was going to require a difficult and dangerous procedure. Mom went to Tucson, flying for the first time, to be on hand to assist. That left Dad and me. He found me a job at a garage in Medina, and I rode in with him every morning to work. It was a boring job; among other duties, such as counting all the tires of various sizes in stock, I had to measure daily how much gasoline was still in the storage tank. I seldom got it right. I taught Dad how to play chess. It was a mistake. He took such a liking to it that I had to play with him almost every night.

Lu delivered her baby on September, 1948, a little girl they named Sharon. There were no near tragedies. Mom came home. I was still in Chippewa when it came time to vote. I had been actively supporting Henry Wallace and Glen Taylor in their campaign for president and vice-president on the Progressive Party ticket. In that effort they had the full support of Paul Robeson. I was not registered in Ohio, but because I was living with my parents and working in the county seat, I was allowed to vote. Later, my father told me he had been informed that I was the only person in Chippewa who voted for Wallace. So much for the secret ballot!

I had a letter from Ernie saying he would be at a conference in Cleveland and would like to see me. I arranged to go to Cleveland, saying I was going to visit a cousin who lived there. I met Ernie instead, to the great joy of both of us. By the time the weekend was over, I had resolved to go back to New Jersey and face whatever problems there were. I left my old home within a week or two and returned to my real home.

I applied for and got a job at District 4 in Newark and resumed living in my house, in my former apartment with my dog, Sally, a Cocker Spaniel I had acquired while in Ohio. Money was so tight I remember worrying every day if I would have 10 cents for a can of food for Sally. The divorce was still stalled. The following February, I found out I had accidentally become pregnant. In 1950 this presented problems. Abortions were messy, illegal, expensive and dangerous. I knew that many times women who had had them could never bear children. I could not accept that course of action and never gave any thought to not having my baby, but how to do it? I visited one home for unwed mothers, but the director and I agreed that since I was independent and resourceful, it was not the place for me. Ernie was neutral. There was not one single person on my side. How did I counter all the criticism? I lied. I was known to be a truthful person, so when I said my doctor had told me it was too late for me to have a safe abortion, I was believed.

Suddenly, we were at war in Korea. The atmosphere in our country changed abruptly. I was scheduled to distribute leaflets opposing the war early one morning at a G.M. shop in Linden. I still had to put on my coat when the knock came on the door, but by the time I got downstairs the car had gone. The whole group was arrested that day.

I had been accustomed to canvassing for progressive causes, but it became very uncomfortable, if not dangerous.

In the summer of 1949, Robeson attended the Paris Peace Conference. He was one of the speakers and he said:

> We in America do not forget that it was on the backs of white workers from Europe and on the backs of millions of blacks that the wealth of America was built. And we are resolved to share it equally. We reject any hysterical raving that urges us to make war on anyone. Our will to fight for peace is strong... We shall support peace and friendship among all nations, with the Soviet Union and the People's Republics.

Before he had even started to speak, the Associated Press (AP) put out word that Paul had said: "It is unthinkable that American Negroes would go to war on behalf of those who have oppressed us for generations against the Soviet Union which in one generation has lifted our people to full human dignity."

This lie caused a nationwide storm of anger against Paul. A concert that had been scheduled for him in August in Peeksville, N.Y., where he had sung three times before, was attacked and prevented. This could not be tolerated. Another concert, scheduled for September, was arranged. Progressives, union members and ordinary people who believed such Hitler-like tactics were wrong got ready to attend. Ernie drove off with Joe Squires, telling Bobby and me that we should stay home. So of course we found a bus going there and got on it. Over 20,000 people attended. We were disturbed by a helicopter flying overhead, and we later learned that at least one sniper's nest had been found. There were speeches. Paul sang, guarded by hundreds of ex-servicemen in uniform and by union members. Pete Seeger sang. As we started for home, trouble erupted. Hundreds of people lining the exit roads for miles started pelting cars with rocks, breaking windows and injuring those leaving the concert, even pulling people from cars and beating them while police stood by. Bobby and I found our husbands and returned with them in their car, luckily escaping injury.

A year later, in 1950, Paul's passport was revoked under the McCarran Act, over his work against imperialism and what the State Department called his "frequent criticism while abroad of the treatment of blacks in the United States."

In the meantime, another kind of blow struck me personally. I was unexpectedly and unequivocally told that because I was pregnant, I must leave Hudson County. A room was found for me with a white family near Weequahic Park in Newark. Within days I left my house, my apartment, my dog, my things and Ernie drove me to my new home.

I continued working at District 4 but took on additional part-time work. The UE was being raided by a right-wing upstart union called the International Union of Electrical Workers (IUE). Each new raid of a local required the institution of suit. A heavy load fell on

Morton Stavis, the union's lawyer. He needed help. I was carrying a big burden with the Jersey City house and needed money. I began going to his office after work and pitching in. I liked him, and he was grateful for my assistance. Jim McLeish, the president of District 4, was among the most decent men I have ever encountered. He allowed me to continue work until shortly before I was due to give birth. I spent the last six weeks happily walking in the park, laying in a modest layette, reading about the birth process (but not yet about caring for babies) and living for the rare visits Ernie could make to Newark. Before giving birth, I was told that when I left the hospital, I would go to a new room, this time with a black family, Arthur and Virgie Dyer. They were kind to me. I did not know whom to designate to take care of my child if I should not live and finally picked that childless couple whom I was sure was married. A year or so later, I had to find something for Virgie. She told me to look in her bureau drawer. I did and to my astonishment, found among the lingerie a marriage certificate dated a few days prior to the day I had given birth.

I awoke early on a beautiful, sunny Sunday morning in October, with labor pains. Arthur drove me to Irvington General Hospital where I spent a fairly happy day until serious labor began. The baby was born that evening. It was a girl. I complained about the time of her arrival, saying she had made me miss dinner, but I was in seventh heaven. She was beautiful and I named her Mindy Jennifer for my mother Minnie and Ernie's mother Jenny. Later we learned that she had a dislocated hip. By the time she was two weeks old, she was in the care of an orthopedist. How did I manage to pay for all this? I had been covered by the group insurance program at District 4 and Katherine Hoffman, director of the plan, continued to cover me for a decent interval, a kind and courageous thing for her to do. (She did have one selfish motive. She was hoping that when things settled down I would come to work for her.)

Coming to motherhood, as I did, without ever having taken care of children or given any thought to the subject, I nevertheless approached it as an exciting new experience. Mindy's dislocated hip required lots of extra care. She had to wear a kapok-filled pad between her legs to position that hip properly. It had to be buckled on after each diaper change. And never a morning arrived with her still wearing it. It was uncanny how she managed to wiggle out. We had been home from the hospital only a few days when a hurricane struck New Jersey. It was one of five to occur in the U.S. in October 1950, something of a record. The electricity went out, the furnace went out, one of our windows blew out, the diaper service failed to deliver, and everything in the house was wet. During the days we all pretty much lived in the kitchen, huddled around the gas range. We ate up everything in the house. Nights we went to bed early and hunkered down to keep as warm as possible. We worried about our littlest resident, but she came through without a sniffle or a complaint.

Ernie visited us on Ridgewood Avenue whenever he was in town. A factory worker for 19 years, he had organized his shop into an independent union, then taken it into the burgeoning CIO's electrical workers' union, the UE, and then he had been asked to join the staff of the UE, becoming the first black to work for an international union. When first hired, he had been told that he could not organize white workers, only black workers. He proved this was not true and went on to become known as "Big Train" for his ability to bring home the desired results in contract negotiations with GE and Westinghouse, among others. He was much in demand for the heavy lifting, was called on to travel widely across the country, and was seldom in Essex County.

His main responsibility was as secretary of the union's Fair Practices Committee, in which capacity he sought to build a coalition of white and black workers to fight for better conditions for all but also to improve the status of the black workers. He found the women workers most willing to work together since they were also held down to the lowest jobs and had difficulty advancing.

Notable among his achievements at this period was the key role he played in the first national organization of black trade unionists, known as the National Negro Labor Council. He was the Director of Organization, working with outstanding black labor leaders from the UAW, Mine-Mill, Rubber, Chemical and other unions. The NNLC's founding convention was held in Cincinnati, Ohio, attended by over 1,000 delegates, representing tens of thousands more. One-third of the delegates were women. White union members who were in sympathy were not excluded. I could not resist. I convinced Arthur Dyer to drive two or three union members and me from Jersey City to the convention in his old Cadillac, a wonderfully smooth-riding car but with problematic brakes. It was hard to leave Mindy but she was in Virgie's hands and safe. The convention was thrilling, full of new ideas, new hope, and new determination. Paul Robeson was the key speaker and brought the house down. Ernie as director of organization held it all together, and his speech was a rousing address calling for "a new wind of freedom." I was touched by his finding a few hours for me in spite of his leading role. Our daughter later wrote the first history of the NNLC.

I continued to live with the Dyers. It was my hope that I could stay home and take care of Mindy, loving my golden baby, enjoying her, educating her, living on my income of $50 a month and, above all, frantically reading books on how to be a good mother, most especially Dr. Spock, who wrote the bible for child-rearing in those days.

It was during this period that I received a letter from the husband of the white couple from whom I had rented a room in Charlotte while I worked there. His wife had died and he felt free to learn whether I was well and happy. I wrote him back that I was, without details. He had admired me because I was fighting against bigotry. Quite out of the blue, he came to Newark to see me. He must have been surprised to find me with a baby but he took it in stride, expressed his pleasure that I had found happiness, and again told me how much he admired me for the stand I was taking. He was a good man and I hold him in high regard in my memory, the more so because he was Southern born and bred.

I was invited by my parents to take a trip with them to visit my sister in Arizona. I could not refuse and felt safe with Mindy in Virgie's care. I went to Ohio and from there we drove to Arizona. I never failed to enjoy Tucson, hunting enthusiastically for Indian artifacts and adding to my collection of rugs, vases and baskets. The highlight of the trip for me was a visit to the Grand Canyon. Dad, Lu and I went down on mules. It was a long and scary trip; I think this infidel prayed all the way. All that had to happen was for the mule to have his back, rather than his head, to the canyon. He could then lose his sense of direction and go over. On a lighter note, there were rest stations along the way. Each mule would move up, relieve himself while the ones behind waited their turn, and then move on. None of this means that I don't have a picture in my head of the splendid colors of the rocks and the magnificent size of the canyon, truly one of the wonders of the world.

It was not until a year or so later, when my parents came east on a trip and I saw them on the Jersey shore, that I told my mother about the baby I had named for her. She was moved to tears and responded lovingly, even finding a gift for us in her slim wallet.

At Christmas, I went to the UE party where I ran into Mort. We danced and he asked if I could help out in his office for two weeks. I said yes, hired Virgie to take care of Mindy and reported to work, unaware that Mort's situation had changed. The IUE's plunder of the UE had desiccated his practice to the point where he could no longer support his own office. He had joined his brother-in-law, Joel Gross, in his practice at 744 Broad Street, Newark. From working class clients in a few small offices in an unassuming, undistinguished building to rich and influential clients and a suite of elegant offices in the most prestigious building in Newark~a block from Broad and Market, then the busiest intersection in the country~was a big leap, but Mort was a man at home in all environments and with all clients. Besides its regular caseload, the office was now representing the State of Israel to qualify it to issue Israel Bonds in the U.S., a unique honor and a weighty responsibility. Mort was in charge of the project.

At the end of two weeks, I was offered a permanent job and had to make a decision. Was I simply going back to work fulltime? Practical considerations prevailed, and I went to work. I felt at a disadvantage with the other women in the office. I got a new permanent, had my hair dyed a becoming red-blonde and thought longingly about buying better clothes. It couldn't last. I was earning $50 a week and paying Virgie $25, besides carrying the Jersey City expenses. I soon returned to straight brown hair and being plain. I was to stay at that job for 42 years.

Mort having recently reacquired Thelma Oster, the secretary he had had in D.C., I was assigned as secretary to Martin Kurasch until he moved to the national office of Israel Bonds, and then to Samuel Koenigsberg. Both of them had formerly been with the Securities & Exchange Commission. They were easy to work with and I became devoted to each turn. In an unexpected turn of events, Thelma met a man, fell in love and in two weeks decided to marry. They did so with Mort's blessing, whereupon he co-opted me. The Israel Bond campaign was launched and our work became litigation.

When Mindy was two, she and I took the train to New York, then the subway uptown to wherever the May Day parade was to begin, and walked block after block back down to 14th Street where that glorious event ended, she riding in my flimsy $10 stroller and I pushing. She was very game, never crying or complaining the entire day.

While living back home in Ohio, I had acquired a cocker spaniel puppy and the Dyers had graciously allowed me to bring my dog, Sally, with me. Sally, following my example, became pregnant. She proved to be uncooperative by going into labor in the middle of the night, but I was undeterred. I roused Mindy from sleep, put a jacket on her and took her to the back porch to watch the puppies arrive. She did not seem to find it as miraculous as I did, and I'm afraid it did nothing to prepare her for her career as a doctor. She did have a relationship with the dog. I once found her under the kitchen table having a wonderful time chewing on a juicy bone put down for Sally and Sally not objecting.

Since I had almost no money to spend on toys and entertainment for my daughter, I invented the Name Game. Wherever we were, I would point to an object and tell her its name. The next time I pointed to it, I expected her to know it,

5.3 Maggie with baby Mindy

and she almost always did. Thus, at one and a half, she knew the word windowsill, not to mention doorknob, Venetian blind, fire escape, traffic light, etc. I did not know how to talk to babies, so I talked to her in my natural vocabulary. Sometimes she modified the words a little. She often told me of something she had learned that was "insterting." And she found going to "Bangebber's" store a real treat.

I continued to live with the Dyers and Virgie continued to take care of Mindy. In 1953, fate in the form of Urban Renewal decreed that we had to move from Ridgewood Avenue so that it could be transformed, into what and for what purpose we were never told. Arthur found an apartment on Ward Street in Orange and we moved there.

ENTRE'ACTE
COUSINS

Dad's relatives never came to visit us; Mom's did. I remember one Thanksgiving weekend when the house was so full that there was talk of having someone sleep on the ironing board. I was very young and that worried me. It would be hard, not at all comfy and it was too tall. Suppose you fell off?

And Mom's brother Fred, who had four wives in succession but no kids, was the only one who ever remembered us at Christmas. He always sent presents. Two successive years they were the same—fountain pens that leaked. But we were always reminded that it was the thought that mattered.

So our cousins that are remembered are from Mom's side. I keep telling myself to go on Ancestors.com and find Dad's family but have not done it. Thus, all I can write about are my sister's descendants.

SHARON REISER THRALL

Sharon was Lu's and Jim's firstborn. I first met her when she was three and thought then that she was the most attractive and charming child ever. She was. And she has remained as lovable. My next contact with her was as a college student when I was delegated to help her find an appropriate dress for my parents' 50th wedding celebration. We had a chance to talk and I learned that she was participating in the protests against the Vietnam War, which surprised me in light of her parents' conservatism, and, needless to say, provided a bond between us. Even then Sharon knew where she was going with her life: medicine. From her high school days she was a member of a group that regularly went into the mountains surrounding Tucson to rescue hikers or hunters.

She went to both college and medical school at the University of

E 2.1 Lu's Family: First row: Don and Sharon. Second row: Danielle, Bryan, John, Erin, Sierra

Arizona. She fell in love, married Greg Thrall, and moved to Oregon to practice her profession, settling in Roseburg. Roseburg is a city in southern Oregon on the Umpqua River, with what seems like an ideal climate averaging between 80 degrees in the summer and 30 in the winter. It has a population of about 21,000, almost all white. The surrounding countryside is wooded, mountainous, and scenic. They are close enough to the Pacific Ocean to enjoy it on vacations.

Sharon and her husband had two children, Bryan and Erin, and then divorced. Sharon continued to practice medicine. She is the kind of doctor who instills complete confidence in her patients. Her present field is Urgent Medicine. For many years she owned a magnificent place on the Umpqua, including a large house and a lot covered with huge evergreen trees. She is now in the process of selling it and in the meantime has moved to smaller quarters in town.

DON JAMES REISER

Then Jim and Lu had Don, named for his father and his grandfather. Like them, he has always had good looks, a pleasant disposition, lots of ability and the willingness to work hard. He went to school at the University of Arizona for two years, leaving to start a restaurant business with a friend. He then began working for the Tack Troom, Tucson's exclusive restaurant, where he was a waiter, a manager and the maitre d' for years, jobs demanding much diplomacy and stamina. He was married young and divorced young.

When Jim died and Lu decided to move to Oregon, Don also made the move in order to be near and helpful to his mother. He got a job in a factory run by Orenco, a company with a world-wide business manufacturing solid waste management systems. Within two years he was promoted to being one of three shift supervisors. When the recession hit, the factory laid everybody off except for a skeleton crew.

Roseburg now has 12-15% unemployment, making it impossible to find a job. Don's present plan is to sell his house and return to his beloved Tucson.

BRYAN ALDEN THRALL

Bryan was the firstborn of Sharon and her husband. He had a rocky start but with his parents' devoted care and sensible attitude, has become an outstanding example of good health and ability. He attended Washington University in St. Louis where he majored in Computer Sciences, going on to get his Master's degree. His first job was with a flight simulator company called FlightSafety, writing software that draws the graphics the pilots see out the windows of the flight simulator. He continues in this vitally necessary work.

For a few years while he was in school Bryan and I corresponded. One of the ways he endeared himself to me was his habit of ending his letters with this poem:

Had I the heavens' embroidered cloths,
Enwrought with golden and silver light,
The blue and the dim and the dark cloths
Of night and light and the half-light,
I would spread the cloths under your feet:
But I, being poor, have only my dreams;
I have spread my dreams under your feet;
Tread softly because you tread on my dreams.[1]

Bryan takes care of his health, swimming and working out. In 2008 he was married to Danielle Slone. His mother Lu was then ill so I was drafted to attend and had the pleasure of participating as the great aunt at their splendid wedding. Danielle is a school teacher and recently completed work on her Master's. As 2011 dawned they had the great pleasure of welcoming their first child, a little blue-eyed girl named Maggie Erin. There is not a doubt in the world that Maggie Erin is lucky in being born to a couple who will be superb parents, assuring her a happy life. There is also no doubt that to the extent she is named in part for me, I am gratified and pleased and happy.

E 2.2 Maggie Erin

ERIN THRALL NUNES

Erin has always been an exceptional young woman, venturing into unusual areas. She became an automobile mechanic and a motorcyclist. In England she worked in a stable.

She then became a firefighter and an EMT and, while still fighting fires, has progressed to being a paramedic.

1   "He Wishes For The Cloths Of Heaven" by William Butler Yeats.

She has always been tall, strong and stunningly attractive but combines this with the same sweetness and consideration that characterize her brother. Her education included one year abroad as an exchange student in Germany. She then went to junior college and to John Hancock, a firefighting school. Curious, daring and courageous would seem to be the words to best describe her.

Now she is remarried, the mother of Sierra, a little girl born September 4, 2009, and with her husband John is expecting another child in the fall.

VI
ORANGE, THE EARLY YEARS
(1953-1958)

The summer we moved to Orange, Mindy had one of her usual bouts of tonsillitis, and penicillin was prescribed for her over the phone by Dr. Leonard Tushnet, my doctor, who had delivered her and taken care of her from birth. She took the medicine but continued to get worse. I gave more medicine, and she got even worse. Finally, with both of us in tears, I called the doctor again and described her condition. Within half an hour, he was at our door. She had developed an allergy to penicillin and was near death. He pulled her through but she was not able to take that antibiotic again. I was so frightened that I bought her a bracelet to wear all the time, warning against her allergy.

I found a highly regarded day care center that agreed to take children her age, and Mindy started school two days before her second birthday. It snowed early that year. I felt sorry for her and carried her to the bus. That bus took us to another bus that took us to a designated corner where we stood and waited for her to be picked up. I then caught a bus to work, arriving half an hour before I was scheduled to start. This became our daily routine and we adapted to it. She liked the nursery, and I felt she was getting the best education I could manage. The problem was at the other end of the day when I was sometimes kept late. The van delivering Mindy home was never late. It became a daily worry because the driver once left my two-year-old outdoors, alone. She was in a panic by the time I arrived.

It was about this time that I began to feel I was never going to be able to marry Ernie and had better look to the future. After considerable thought, I determined to move to Hawaii, confident that both Mindy and I would do well there. Mort was taking steps to help me get a job with Harry Bridges, head of the longshore union, when Ernie said, "Stick around." I was still head-over-heels in love.

"Veni, Vidi, Velcro."[1]

6.1 Mindy's 3rd birthday

Mindy and I spent a lot of time in Orange Park, a few blocks from where we were living. I began to look at the houses on Olcott, a street three blocks long bordering the park, and found one near Highland Avenue. I consulted a real estate agent and was shown a number of houses but always remembered that one, finally signing a contract in early summer of 1953 to buy it for $9,700. Orange Savings Bank discriminated against me because I was a woman and a widow, granting me only 15 years instead of the usual 30-year deal. It was a hardship but not a single payment was late or missed.

The very day the contract was signed, I went home to our one room on Ward Street and stayed up late packing everything we owned. I sold the Jersey City house but the closing on Olcott Street was delayed until November 6, 1953, by requests from the former owners. I was so buoyed up that I cheerfully lived out of boxes for five or six months.

The day after the closing, I rented a truck and, with Mindy bouncing along on the seat beside me, drove to Ward Street where Arthur and some friends loaded our stuff—Mindy's crib, her chest of drawers and toys, a refrigerator, a double bed, another chest of drawers, our clothes and books and not much else —delivered them the few blocks to the new house and unloaded them.

6.2 397 Olcott St.

397 Olcott was one of the houses constructed cheaply after WWII to meet the housing shortage. Its right-hand neighbor was a standard large house; its left a copy of itself. The small stoop at the front door had steps and a walk leading straight

---

1   "I came, I saw, I stuck around." Thanks to Paul Violi for a line from one of his poems.

down to the sidewalk. There was a comfortably sized backyard with an elm tree and a maple. Behind our property was a woods owned by the city. The house itself was one-story with an attic that could be improved. There were small windows throughout. There were two bedrooms, a kitchen and a bathroom. A set of stairs led to a basement with a large coal-burning furnace. There was a door in the kitchen leading to the backyard. There was a bare minimum of shrubbery.

Once installed on Olcott St., I began a long-delayed effort to make a happy home. Mindy's room, already papered appropriately for a child, was soon complete. The bedroom I chose was half complete. We had no living room furniture except for a set of three round stools with cast iron legs. The kitchen had our refrigerator, a stove, of course, and I found a card table. I don't remember what we sat on, but on our first night in the new house we had a gala dinner with Murl Daniels, a young woman I had met at a local YWCA dance class who volunteered to help and became a dear, dear friend for the rest of her too short life. After Murl left, I prepared for bed. We had been cleaning and cooking all day. When I stopped to wash my face before bed, I turned on the hot water. Steam rushed out and filled the room. I called the Fire Department. They arrived in minutes and found that the hot water heater was on and there was no cutoff valve to turn it off. We would have had an explosion in a few minutes. I thought it was an irresponsible thing for the sellers to do and regretted that I had been lenient with them about vacating the house.

Before long I ventured to Bamberger's (a major department store in Newark) and purchased a lovely sofa, one easy chair and a dinette table and chairs. Thanksgiving and Christmas being only two months away, I also acquired enough things for simple celebrations on those holidays. With the addition of two sturdy wicker arm chairs sent to us by Sam Koenigsberg, the attorney in Mort's office with whom I had the pleasure of working for a few years, we were at home.

I bought a used Rolleiflex that Mort located for me for $120. It had a Zeiss lens and its product was quite superb. I became an avid photographer. A favorite thing to do was to take a day off from work once a year and spend it at whatever nursery school Mindy was attending, shooting not only her but as many children as I could. I

6.4 Girls hanging laundry

would later give enlarged copies of the pictures to the school.

When Mindy was three, Dan Crystal was hired as an attorney in our office and moved his family to East Orange from Washington, D.C. He had an angel wife, Frances, two boys, Steve and Roy, and a four-year-old daughter named Sally. Mindy and Sally became best friends and have remained close to this day. The best memories of Mindy's young life revolve around their house on Maple Avenue and her experiences when she was chosen as a companion for Sally on camping trips.

That same year, I borrowed Sam's car for some errands. A small accident occurred. Another driver drove into us. I saw it coming and froze. No one was injured and only slight damage was done to Sam's

FROM ONE TO NINETY-ONE – A LIFE

6.5 Raymond and Mindy moving blocks

car, but I concluded that my reaction had not been the right one—I should have speeded up or backed up or screamed or blown the horn or something. I concluded I was not a safe driver and never drove again.

Ernie's divorce finally came through, leaving him furious at the heavy alimony and child support payments imposed. He had achieved an enviable position. From being a factory worker for 19 years, he had become the only black member of the national staff of the UE and one of its top negotiators, but the UE had a policy of not paying its organizers more than the wages paid in the shops they organized. He was making $75 a week, with an extra $5 for expenses, in a day when a hamburger in any restaurant near the national office cost that amount. He paid as much and as often as he could and his ex-wife was very decent, managing on that and her job, and not harassing him.

We were married on January 8, 1954, in a Methodist Church in Newark. I borrowed a dress that was both stunning and becoming, and Sam gave me a camellia, rare and beautiful. Mindy was down with tonsillitis, so Sam's wife Muriel babysat. Mort and Esther gave us a wedding reception

6.3 Ernie and Maggie's wedding picture

attended by a generous number of our friends. By the time the party was over, I was ill with the flu. Someone took me home in a car without a heater. Ernie went to his own place for the night. I was very sick for the following week.

Ernie came to visit, was dismayed at the house's not having taller ceilings and disappointed at seeing how small it was. He also took pains to explain to me that I would never come first in his life-the liberation of his people took first place. When I was well, I returned to work and came home one day to find he had moved in. His first act was to burn all my letters in the furnace.

He was home one day when I started looking for a cigarette. I could not find any in the house and went to the closet to see if he had some in his coat pockets. Instead of smokes I found a letter from a woman with whom he had been having an affair, explaining to him why she thought it was fairer for him to wed me since there was already a child. I went to the park in spite of the bitter cold and walked and wept until I was calm. I was furious to realize that while I was selling a house, buying a house, taking care of Mindy and financing the whole operation to make a home for us, he was philandering.

Another problem soon became apparent. Mindy, having lived all her life under the name Hunter, believed Cliff had been her father. She resisted changing that belief, refusing to accept Ernie as her father. I had trouble understanding this and more trouble trying to deal with it. Up to then, I thought she was an easy child to raise and I enjoyed her young years tremendously. One problem I remember. When she was nearly three, she liked to take off all her clothes and walk around outside wearing only my high heeled shoes. I have a photo to prove it.

As soon as we could afford it, we arranged for Joe Squires, who had been of inestimable help in making the Jersey City house fit to live in, to improve our house on Olcott Street. He demolished the wall between the living room and bedroom on the first floor, put two bedrooms in the attic, moved the backdoor to the side of the house, repositioned the stairway to the basement, and--best of all--replaced the two small front windows with a huge picture window extending the length of the living room. It took a long time. Joe had to work between assignments for the union. We got used to living with part of the house torn-up. I remember one time while the roof was open to build the attic, a terrible lightning and rain storm hit. Ernie spent the night on the roof holding down tarpaulins to keep us dry. But when it was finished, what a treat! The only near tragedy we experienced occurred when Josh, who was two, stuck a screwdriver in an electric outlet and was booted across the floor.

The political life of our country took some turns. The Cold War became more intense. In 1950, Julius and Ethel Rosenberg had been arrested, the "first victims of American fascism." They were charged with having given the Soviet Union the secret of the atomic bomb, an obviously impossible thing for them to have done, but the administration found them guilty. They had many supporters. For years we petitioned, protested, picketed. In fact, there was such widespread feeling in favor of their innocence that the government had no choice. The Rosenbergs had to die. The administration could not tolerate the years of mounting protest to be expected if they had simply been jailed. They were executed on June 19, 1953.

From being legal, the Communist Party became illegal. Twelve national leaders were prosecuted and tried, charged only with conspiring to *teach* the overthrow of the government by force and violence. They were found guilty and jailed. If I remember correctly, the news came the same day as the world was being beguiled by the marriage of Princess Elizabeth in England. Few people knew or cared that the entire leadership of a once free and legal political party was going to prison. Now, in 2011, with all the publicity about Kate and William and the royal wedding another effort is being made to take our minds off the serious problems facing this nation. As Yogi Berra said, it is deja vu all over again.

My conviction that socialism is the only solution to the problems of living together in peace was ravaged, but not demolished, by the stories that came out after the death of Stalin in 1953 about the undemocratic nature of socialism as practiced in the USSR. I still kept the friends I had made in the progressive movement, but more and more Ernie became my political and theoretical leader.

Mindy should have started kindergarten, but there was none at Oakwood, the only school she could enter. Oakwood was in the ghetto. The only kindergarten was at Heywood, the white community next to us on the hill, and it took children at four. I estimate that the two-year delay caused because her school had no kindergarten cost us an extra $1,200 in nursery school fees, a heavy tax on our working class family.

Every Spring there was an additional cost we had to meet. In the community where we lived, it was the custom for every child to have an Easter outfit, brand-new from top to bottom. I rather enjoyed this annual shopping with Mindy and she never failed to look lovely in her new finery. One year Josh got into the act. He was about nine or 10 and had decided he, too, wanted a new outfit. I complied. He was up at the crack of dawn on Easter Sunday and fully togged out. Without warning, it started to rain. We got through the day, but the weather dampened the

6.6 Easter finery

triumph Josh was hoping for.

In December of 1955 a remarkable~a revolutionary~thing had happened. Rosa Parks sat down on a bus and, when told to move back "where she belonged," still sat. The whole world is familiar with what happened next: the bus boycott, thousands of blacks walking to work daily, King's home bombed, a hundred leaders of the boycott sent to jail, and King's philosophy of non-violence winning many whites to the struggle, including President Johnson. In December 1956, segregation was outlawed on Montgomery busses, but it would not be until 1964 that a national Civil Rights Act was passed.

When Mindy's fifth Christmas came, I had put a great deal of thought into the best presents for her. There were five of them for a total cost of $25. That was a lot of money. I customarily fed the family on less than that for a week. It was not a cheerful holiday, and it seemed to me that for the good of all of us we had to have another child. Ernie already had two from his first marriage, a daughter named Beverly and a son named for his father and called "Brumpy." Beverly had been used in the divorce trial to testify against Ernie. He maintained her testimony was false, and he never forgave her.

He did keep in touch with Brumpy, was fond of him and enjoyed his company. Brumpy, now in his late 60's, has lived an interesting life, clever enough to make his living at the race track. As might be expected he has two handsome and brainy children, Geanine and Michael.

In short, Ernie was not eager to have more children, but I was determined and he did not object. I was still working with Sam when I started carrying our second child. Like the first pregnancy, I was healthy except that this time, towards the end, the baby began to lie on the sciatic nerve in my right hip. Walking to the bus every morning was so painful that I would be in tears. I stopped work on a Friday, pains started on Sunday and Dr. Tushnet told me to go to one of the Newark hospitals. The pains stopped, but I stayed on through Monday and Tuesday before finally giving birth on a Wednesday in June, 1956, to a healthy and vigorous boy. I suggested we name the baby Joshua Paul for his paternal grandfather and Paul Robeson, and Ernie agreed.

There was a soft, warm rain that night. I sat at an open window rejoicing and reading. The next morning I could not get out of bed. I had caught cold in all the muscles involved in giving birth and had to stay in the hospital an extra week. So did Josh. I could not nurse, having injured one nipple in a game effort, without instruction, to nurse Mindy. At every meal time, the cart with the babies could be heard coming down the hall, with Josh crying the loudest. He was big and being starved. When that was remedied, he no longer had to scream. Before I left the hospital, I wrote a detailed account of the discrimination I experienced at the hands of its employees simply because I had a tan baby. I never received an acknowledgment or apology.

For the greater part of our first two years in Orange, Ernie was traveling, doing the Fair Practices work for which he was chairman, in short, fighting discrimination in whatever form he found it in the union or the companies involved. He also did time and motion studies to prevent speed-up. But increasingly he was asked to handle top-level negotiations. We saw him whenever he got back East, and we took great pleasure in his visits. But it was clear that McCarthyism was growing and that the UE might have to retrench.

Our coal-burning furnace, while it existed (we later converted to gas) became popular during the McCarthy period. Progressives who felt threatened and had much to lose brought their once-loved libraries to us for disposal. We often kept a volume or two we had coveted but could not afford. The balance we burned with apologies to the spirit of the U.S. Constitution and *Fahrenheit 451*.

It was about this time that the FBI began to harass us, parking in the street across from our house every morning and staying there for hours, interviewing our neighbors, stopping me when I left work at the end of a long day, even visiting my dad in Ohio. He told me about it later and simply said he had told them I had a right to think as I pleased.

Six weeks after Josh was born, Ernie came home with the news that he had received the "unkindest cut of all." His special local in Hoboken at the Keufel & Esser plant-the one closest to his heart, with more than usually intelligent workers making a sophisticated product, slide rules, and where he had a close relationship with the president of the local, Fred Korman, and had made substantial gains in wages and conditions for the members--had yielded to the red scare and voted to leave the UE. This was happening more and more so that the National Office had no choice but to cut staff. Ernie was out of a job. He was immediately offered one with the rival IUE. Several of the laid-off UE organizers were taking those offers. We decided it would be an unprincipled thing to do since he would be unable to carry on his fair practices work and the programs he was initiating to advance the cause of women workers.

That weekend we held a previously scheduled barbecue for Paul Robeson, whose passport had been revoked in 1950 under the McCarran Act over his work against imperialism and what the State Department called his "frequent criticism while abroad of the treatment of blacks in the US." There were eight long years when the government attempted to leave him without an income. It pretty much succeeded. Paul had made his living through concerts but was finding that no one in the U.S. would allow him access to a hall. He needed

6.7 Robeson BBQ

money. Paul and Ernie had known each other since their teen years. In 1954, Ernie had organized a committee and I rented a hall in Newark, but when I went to sign the contract, I was told they had not realized who Robeson was. There was no way they could rent to him.

Now Ernie was again undertaking to build support for Paul, hoping it would lead to renting a hall and conducting a concert. On the Friday evening before the barbecue, he took him around to the local watering places like the Harmony Bar so that folks could get to know and like him. On Saturday the barbecue took place. It was a gala affair. I had spent hours cleaning the house and the yard, setting up the lawn furniture, arranging an area for playing horse shoes. Fran Crystal brought flowers to decorate the tables. The affair started with a parade led by "Seneca" Charles Millis in his tribal garb, riding Buck. The most famous of the local cooks presided at the grill, and friends brought an abundance of delicious dishes. There was beer. And good cheer and high hopes for a new day.

Midway through the afternoon, Paul held Josh in his arms and sang "Joshua fit the battle of Jericho." It was a dedication and a christening. Years later when Josh established his recording studio, he called his company Tallest Tree Music in tribute to Robeson, who was known as "The Tallest Tree in the Forest."

The committee continued to meet and work for the next year but never had success. Paul had no relief until 1958 when his passport was restored and he could travel freely and earn a living. The years of persecution had taken a terrible toll on his health.

Ernie started looking for work. He was hopeful, knowing he had well-developed people skills. He began seeking employment at Bamberger's, without luck. He applied to be a salesman for some of the big liquor manufacturers, without luck. He networked, without luck. He was becoming discouraged about finding a job but in the meantime, I became increasingly outraged as it was more and more clear that the Oakwood School Mindy was attending was an inferior jim crow school with second-hand textbooks. We obtained a copy of the map of the school districts. It showed a line running through the middle of Orange Park~right in front of our door~sending the white children east of the park to Heywood, even bussing them there, and sending the black children west of the park to Oakwood, *sans* bussing.

Brown v. Board of Education had been upheld by the U.S. Supreme Court in 1954, making *de jure* segregation in schools illegal. Kelly Alexander, who had been head of the NAACP when I was living in Charlotte, brought the suit from that state. But it was not until 1957, after years of rioting and finally integration by nine courageous black students of the high school in Little Rock, Arkansas—under the eyes of federal troops—that *de jure* segregation in southern schools began to end.

Ernie organized a committee of parents, analyzed the problem, enlisted the services of the N.J. Division Against Discrimination so it was standing in the wings, skillfully used the local press to expose the shameful situation and rebuffed an attempt to split the parents when the city offered a few black children admission to Heywood. Ernie's word was final: "We fight for *all* the children." Within three months, the fight was won.

During the fight to desegregate the schools, Ernie had become acquainted with Dr. John Alexander who was seriously interested in helping the black community get some power. The Orange government was then made up of five Commissioners elected on a city-wide basis. Ernie convinced Alexander it was impossible to win with only votes in the black ward. Blacks had no influence with the Democratic Party. Its attitude was, "All we have to do is give you liquor and we'll get your votes." Ernie and Alexander set up a meeting with six other black supporters and the white politicians where they stated the old style would no longer work, but the whites did not budge, so they decided to run a candidate and attempt to take some power. Alexander agreed to be the candidate, and a vigorous campaign was run. He did not win, but the people were energized in the process.

This experience convinced Alexander and the others that it was necessary to change the form of government to Mayor-Council, where a representative would be elected from each ward. Ernie led the movement for charter change. Josh at six, as soon as school was over, accompanied him every day in our old car, converted into a sound truck, to spread the word around town. He learned the whole speech and even adopted Ernie's accent and inflections. The referendum passed, thanks to strong support in the East Ward and a coalition Ernie was able to develop with some white residents who also wanted change.

In 1963, Citizens for Representative Government (CRG) successfully ran Benjamin Jones as a candidate for East Ward Councilman and won decisively. CRG then organized for and received the appointment of Dr. John Alexander as the first black chairman of the Board of Education.

During all those years, what was I doing? I thought my life was challenging and exciting. Looking back, I realize it was hard. I worked diligently as the breadwinner. Mort kept me on a small salary, but I never considered leaving because I knew he would not fire me if the House Un-American Activities Committee came breathing down my neck, which was happening to numerous law-abiding citizens, including a number I knew. Until he lost his job, Ernie was constantly traveling and I had to assume all the duties that needed to be done. It became a pattern.

Money was tight. It was incumbent upon me to do all the shopping in order not to waste a penny. We were often in between cars, second-hand ones tending not to last. The delivery service at the local supermarket was expensive. What happened most often was that I would shop after work and carry the parcels home. In those days, wearing high heeled shoes was expected as proper dress for the office. I once wore a pair of sandals to work and was stopped by an attorney from an unrelated office on our floor and told that I was not properly dressed. So I wore the heels and carried the groceries. I remember one nasty fall and one mugging. It was in those same heels that I often carried the kids out of pity.

There was a period when our dryer wore out and could not be fixed. For months I had to take the wash to a laundromat, by cab, and pick it up at the end of the day, again by cab. I was ultimately saved by Mort's wife, Esther, who heard about this and arranged for us to acquire a new dryer.

Cleaning the house had to be fitted in over the weekends. Ernie generally tended the coal-burning furnace in winters and cut the grass in summers, but if his current campaign was heavy, those jobs also fell to me. He usually got the garbage pails to the curb on pickup days. I did all the cooking and all the dishwashing. I remember once starting the dishes at 10:30~we were running late, I had just finished reading to the kids~when I was so tired I started to cry. Ernie came and inquired what was wrong and was sympathetic, but did not offer to finish the job. Shortly after that, however, he took over one troublesome task~ mopping the kitchen floor. With four persons and four animals using it constantly, it was a major problem to keep it clean.

I was the one who spent time with the kids, bathing, dressing, talking with them, reading to them, arranging for music lessons, taking them for outings often and to the doctor when necessary and I fed, bathed, walked the animals, and finagled to get them to the vet when needed.

I took care of allocating what money we had and paying the bills. I remember sitting one Friday night for half an hour trying to decide what to do with an extra 50 cents. I met with the accountant and filed the tax returns. In this regard we were lucky, our needs being met without charge by Milton Zisman, the generous and helpful man who took care of Mort's office accounts and became a lifelong friend. His most extraordinary gift to Ernie's work was to find the money to build the new high school in Orange without cost to the town's citizens. The Zisman family was a blessing in another way. Milt's wife Sylvia was for years the courageous leader of the peace movement in our area during the Vietnam War and after.

After Ernie became involved in Orange politics, my duties were increased to include typing press releases, cutting stencils and running off leaflets in our kitchen after dinner. I also started an archive, saving copies of everything against the day it might be needed for a written record.

During the summers, while the children were away at camp, I used my two-week vacations to tear the house apart, throw out and replace, clean, paint, redecorate, rearrange and reorganize. I found it rejuvenating for me as well as our home.

To Ernie fell the more arduous task of painting the outside of the house. It had been built of green lumber. As a result, the paint would peel. Even though it was a small house, painting it was time-consuming and costly. Ernie had done it twice in the course of five or six years when we became convinced that putting on aluminum siding would be a better course.

I have not mentioned that from my early 30's I was constantly plagued with broken bones. Osteoporosis was not yet commonly known. I kept breaking bones and Dr. Eleby Washington kept fixing them and prescribing a pill composed of what we used to give the chickens–oyster shells. He was a black orthopedist who was becoming acknowledged even in those unenlightened days as the best in New Jersey in his field. I mention him because to this day doctors who have occasion to look at his work comment on how excellent it was. As more became known about the disease, he sent me for testing in New York.

During our darkest days, Ernie and I would often have arguments, and on two or three occasions, I threatened to apply for divorce. He responded that in such a case he would get the children. I knew he was right. Judges and social workers were then totally opposed to anybody but blacks raising black children. Since I would rather have died than lose my children, that always ended the matter. We would soon make up.

Unable to find a job, Ernie tried to earn some money by doing painting jobs, but the only ones he could finance were small. He was eager to undertake bigger jobs but that required a little capital. It happened that my boss had traveled to Italy with his family and had eaten something that caused him to come down with hepatitis. He was dangerously ill and was required to have bed rest for six weeks. During that time I commuted to his home in Elizabeth to receive and deliver work. He gave me an unexpected but welcome bonus of $250, which I immediately deposited in a bank. At last we had a savings account! It was that money which Ernie convinced me to lend him. The painting venture did not make money and our nest egg was lost. A year or so later, Mort and his family spent a long vacation in Europe, during which time I did what I could to hold the practice together. Upon his return he again gave me a bonus, this time of $350, which I promptly banked. Again Ernie borrowed it and again it was lost in another failed attempt to make some money by painting. After that I did not receive any cash bonuses but every year for Christmas was given some IBM stock. That was the only savings we were able to accumulate.

During his infant years, I used to take Josh every morning three doors away to be cared for by a very old, very sweet and very wise grandmother who kept him safe and happy. Mindy sometimes stayed there, too, on school holidays. Josh was much loved, but he did not get the hour-to-hour supervision that had characterized Mindy's first years. He taught himself to talk. One day we heard him say, "Toe pa up," and realized that indeed the toast in the toaster had popped up. We were so busy that no one noticed his next development until

Mindy announced: "Josh is walking." From then on he was off and running and played an important role in our family life.

When Mindy entered kindergarten she had hair I had allowed to grow from her birth. She wore it in braids, not too expertly crafted. The next summer she came in from play one day with her hair drenched in sweat. I grabbed the scissors and cut it all off. I thought it was very becoming but she broke down sobbing and said "I look just like Baby Tears."

About 1960 I enrolled Mindy in art classes after school at the Newark Museum. She learned to ride the bus alone from Tremont Avenue. Twice I left work and went home automatically, forgetting she was there, and had to take a cab back to get her. Both times I was in great trepidation but found her quietly reading on the Museum steps.

When he reached the age of two, Josh was enrolled in nursery school. When he was three, he became sick and a bottle of penicillin was delivered for him and left on the kitchen table. Josh disappeared and so did the medicine. He had drunk the whole bottle and had to be rushed to the hospital to have his stomach pumped. By the time he was four, he was old enough and big enough that he and Mindy could enjoy playing together, which often took the form of turning the wicker chairs upside down and covering them with a bedspread to create a fort or whatever else their imaginations envisioned.

When he was five, I enrolled him in summer camp at the Newark YM-YWCA. He took the bus to Newark with me every morning and learned to swim that summer. I believe it was the following summer he attended summer camp at the YMCA in Orange. He was leaving one day when he saw a bus approaching, ran across the street and was hit. His arm was broken but it was a "green twig" break and he recovered quickly.

Josh was an animal lover. He came in from the park with a tiny black kitten that had been abandoned. There was no arguing with him. We had no cat, we needed a cat and this was going to be our cat. He named him Joe. Joe turned out to be ideal, not needing a lot of special attention or fancy food, getting along amicably with the other pets we began to acquire, doing something unusual in that he took walks with anybody who went to exercise a dog or simply saunter in the park. He had an accident. His tail was caught in a door, necessitating an amputation and leaving it four inches shorter. When he made a kill of a bird or mouse he sometimes proudly brought it in and, meowing loudly, threw it on the kitchen floor. He lived to be old, became very ill and we asked a kindly vet to put him to sleep.

We were not destined to be a one-cat family, being given a Persian and then a pair of Siamese kittens. With four felines, Ernie put his foot down. One had to go. I kept the female Siamese and gave the male to Catherine Korman. As is known, Siamese cats are snugglers. Had Elizabeth's brother remained in the family, she would have snuggled with him. Failing that, I was forever finding her in my lap. After a few years I gave her to the Dalys, but within a few days she was back, having jumped from a second story window. She did not get over wanting to snuggle, so years later I again gave her away, this time to a friend in Newark with instructions never to let her outdoors. She managed to escape, I am sure to come home but, full of contrition, I waited in vain for her reappearance.

Mindy had enjoyed the school fight, but when it was won and she learned she would not be going back to Oakwood but to Heywood "where the white people lived," she never felt at home. She developed itching. It was so bad that on one occasion, while attending summer day camp at a settlement house in West Orange, she fainted. Then came rage, followed by splitting headaches. "I did not feel like hopping to school any more." She read about other children who had desegregated schools but wondered how in the world they had done it. She cried a lot and retreated into day-dreaming for the next five years. I read recently about a woman named Verna Bailey who was the first black woman to go to Ole Miss[2] and who recalls being terrified: "That time… certainly wasn't a pleasant experience for me. My interactions with white people were very, very limited… I thought my life was going to end." This was the reaction of a mature college-age woman. How much more difficult then must it have been for a grade school child! It is a matter of great regret that neither Ernie nor I was sensitive enough to understand what a price we were asking Mindy to pay.

---

2   The University of Mississippi at Oxford.

ENTR'ACTE
HANNAH, MURL AND FRAN

HANNA LACOB MALKIN

E 3.1 Hannah Lacob Malkin

Hannah and I met in Charlotte. She was a case worker for the City and I a group worker for the YWCA. She was my junior by perhaps half a year. She was a graduate of the University of North Carolina at Chapel Hill and already married to Moses Malkin, who had been drafted and was in the Army. She was petite, dark-haired, intellectual and never at a loss for well-chosen words. We became friends almost instantly.

Hannah immediately recognized that I was from the country and abysmally ignorant. She did not hesitate but went to work on me. I would listen raptly and then respond so ignorantly that she often despaired and would give me something more to read. This went on whenever we met, which was fairly often because we sought each other out. She introduced me to socialism. After I made contact with the NAACP, I asked her to join with me in becoming active. We were the first two whites to join the organization in North Carolina and were active as long as I was in Charlotte, and she after I left. She was far ahead of me in knowing the situation in the South, being accustomed to living among blacks, understanding how urgent was the need for progress, being outraged at each new injustice we encountered, and having a scientific approach to the problems.

Hannah told me a joke that I still enjoy. When taking a sponge bath, you wash down as far as possible, then you wash up as far as possible and then you wash possible.

We lost contact after I left Charlotte, but when I moved to New Jersey, I tracked her down, finding her in Connecticut, happily living with Moe, still childless, retired but involved in all aspects of life in her city and caring about developments in the whole world. She came to visit me in Orange, where I had recently bought a house and was living with three-year old Mindy. Seventeen years later, she hosted Mindy's wedding in her house on Martha's Vineyard.

We still correspond. She has lost Moe through death but otherwise sounds very much like my Hannah, still forward looking and with the same uncanny ability invariably to be right in her judgments of society.

MURL PETERS DANIELS

Alas, I can't call Murl Peters Daniels and ask if what I am writing is appropriate. She died prematurely of late onset diabetes and complications on November 26, 2006. I was privileged to speak at her memorial service. I said, "I was friends with Murl for 53 years... it was not always peaceful~if Murl thought you were not doing right, she'd

E 3.2 Murl Peters Daniels

tell you in no uncertain terms. She was unforgettable. Unique. She could do everything she put her mind to, and everything she did, she did well. She had a brilliant mind, a strong body, and an upright character."

I met Murl at a dance class at the jim crow Orange YWCA on Oakwood Avenue. I had just moved to town and was living with the Dyers in an apartment around the corner on Ward Street. We liked each other from the git-go. Murl was tall, big-boned, pleasantly rounded, brown-skinned, pretty and friendly, with an engaging personality, a winning smile, a quick wit, a brook-me-no-nonsense attitude. I was her friend before the evening was out and loved her all the rest of her life.

Perhaps this will help you understand what kind of person she was. A few weeks later I was able to move into the house I had bought on Olcott Street. She was the only person who came to assist me. She played with my three-year-old, helped with unpacking, found something we could cook for dinner, set up a makeshift table and chairs, and turned our first meal into a banquet.

We continued to be friends and a few years later, when she needed a home, she came to live with us in the downstairs bedroom. (We then had two bedrooms on the second floor, one for Ernie and me and one shared by Mindy and Josh.) I remember the rent was $7 a week for her and her tiny poodle. She enriched my life. She helped improve the landscaping around our house; she introduced me to the music of Frank Sinatra; she frequently took over the cooking, much to the joy of the family. She was with us for five years until she inadvertently found a drawing by Mindy of the room she would like to have. It included a doll corner with the note: "If still wanted when room is gotten." Murl made arrangements to move to an apartment in East Orange.

She had started out as a hairdresser and progressed to working in a factory. She was obviously college material and I kept cajoling her to go to school. Upsala College in East Orange announced several full scholarships for African Americans, and I urged her to sign up. She dilly-dallied. I finally became angry and told her there would be an inevitable backlash, and if she failed to take this opportunity, it might never come again. She went to Upsala and became a teacher in Newark for 25 years. During that period she played a critical role in the life of our family, taking over operation of the kidney machine in our home on which Ernie was required to have a treatment several times a week. She was not afraid of anything, could learn to handle any machine—even that one, on which a patient could bleed to death in three minutes—and knew what to do in emergencies. A remarkable lady.

She was remarkable in another way. When she decided it was time to have a child, she got pregnant, went through a ceremony for the benefit of her mother, took the man's name and had the baby, naming him Seth. He flourished into manhood under her care, unspoiled, hip, educated, loving.

Late in life she developed a business that took her on annual trips to the West Coast of Africa. She made money and no longer had to subsist on a teacher's salary. She also joined a sorority with other women of color and enjoyed the social life and community activities of the group. But even with her new financial status and new social contacts, she remained my friend.

FRANCES HALE

I need a string of adjectives as long as my arm to describe Frances Hale Crystal Moss Hale, who has been my stalwart friend for 57 years. We met at her apartment in East Orange when her daughter was four and mine three. As soon as her husband, Dan Crystal, knew his job in Stavis's office was permanent, he moved his family up from Washington, D.C. When we met it was love at first sight, both for the friendship of Sally and Mindy and for that of Fran and me.

E 3.3 Frances Hale

Fran was born in Japan where her father worked for Otis Elevator. The family, including her and two brothers, lived there for 10 years. She was therefore a cosmopolitan person and accepting of other races and religions. She was a Protestant married to a Jew. Mixed marriages were no stranger to her, and she was thus accepting of my marriage. We were close in age~I am five years her senior. Her career was in Early Childhood Education, for which she was eminently fitted. She has Unitarian and/or Quaker sympathies, allowing her mind to be free.

Fran is warm, pretty, animated, and full of energy. She has blue eyes and long brown hair, now turned that shade of white most

106

desirable~really white. She is slim, loves to exercise and retains a youthful ambience. She went to Antioch College and was impressed by its high academic standards, honor system and single standard for men and women. She is democratic, progressive, familiar with socialism, and was active in campaigns to break segregation in Washington, D.C. restaurants in the late 40's and early 50's. Long before it became popular, she became interested in ecology and lives by those principles, sticking by them even during a sustained period when they caused her hardship. She is a fine cook and an enthusiastic gardener. When she has land, she supplies much of her family's need for fresh vegetables and fruit. She cans. She makes jelly. In short, she jams.

Fran is and always has been an excellent driver, has been interested in science all her life, and collects Stangl ware. She loves music, both classical and folk, and plays piano and an autoharp for pleasure and to assist her in leading songs. She is creative. Lately she has discovered that she has great ability in the art of quilting. She constantly produces outstanding quilts.

Fran enjoys being married, having been wedded almost three-fourths of her life to one or another of her three husbands. It was she who divorced the first two, who still loved her. The third appears to be equally devoted. I should note that the reason Hale appears twice in her name is the following. She was born a Hale. At 10, she met and was attracted to a first cousin named Hal, also a Hale. He also liked her. The question of marriage never arose; marrying a first cousin just not being done. That left them free to be bosom friends, sharing confidences not shared with others. Many, many years later, when she was again free and he had lost his wife to illness, there was no longer any reason not to love and marry. They are now celebrating their 16th year together.

As often as she can travel to the East Coast from their winter home in North Carolina or their summer home in Wyoming, she goes out of her way to visit me and is admired and fondly remembered by all who meet her.

She stays close to her three children, all of whom as kids were bright, imaginative, enterprising, and self-reliant. Without exception they have distinguished themselves in their chosen careers. Stephen is a professor at Rutgers University in New Brunswick, N.J., specializing in the study of aging. Roy is an environmentalist specializing in pure water and clean air systems for cities and a well-known photographer. Sara, known as Sally, is an obstetrical nurse who has "caught" more than 500 babies and has recently become known nationally as a quilter. Fran is devoted to her grandson Ben, a recent graduate of Oberlin College.

Above all, Fran is constant and considerate, a never-failing source of comfort, friendship, counsel and strength. When I count my blessings, I count her twice.

VII
ORANGE, THE LATER YEARS
1958-1971

The principal at Heywood, Josh's first school, told me that Josh's IQ was at least as high as Mindy's, which we knew was high. His academic career never had rivaled hers, his talents lying in music. I had a habit of reading to the kids every night, come hell or high water. Mindy became a great reader of everything she could get her hands on, starting in the second grade when she became impatient with the speed with which I was reading and finished that book herself. Josh also became a reader, with catholic tastes ranging from the classics to science fiction to comic books, starting with Superman but moving enthusiastically to Marvel comics--Spiderman, The Fantastic Four, The Hulk. As to television, I felt from what little I had watched that it would not be a good influence on the kids. Therefore, we had no TV. Then I noticed that Mindy always had an errand at a friend's house after dinner. She was sneaking the forbidden fruit! I relented and bought an inexpensive set. In 1957 the space age arrived with a bang in the form of Sputnik, launching the space race. We tried to see it orbiting the earth but never succeeded.

When it became time for the first child to take piano lessons, there was a problem: no piano. Murl helped solve it. Bamberger's announced a piano sale to start at 6:30 in the morning on a winter Saturday. She and I were there, standing in the cold half an hour early. When the doors opened, you did not leisurely shop for your piano, you raced to the nearest one and held on to it. Thus, for $25 we acquired an elderly upright whose make I do not remember. It sufficed for a few years. Then we bought a new Yamaha upright which filled our needs for the next period. When it became apparent music was going to be Josh's vocation, I bought a Steinway studio grand for $1,000 and gave Mindy the Yamaha, which she still owns. When I sold the house, I sold the Steinway for double what I had paid. In 1998 I bought Josh another grand piano with my final $5,000.

While the children were growing up, we were getting to know Ernie's family. They were solid God-fearing, middle-class, hard-working folks from Maryland and Pennsylvania with intelligence and charm. And, best of all, they welcomed me and my children into the family. We spent one Thanksgiving with his favorite sister, Lorraine Jones, and her family, and they came to visit us over the years. His favorite cousin, Clara Cooper, from Swarthmore, came to see us, and we visited her and her family. Delores, a young niece, came to live with us one summer for several weeks and would have continued except that Ernie's son from his first marriage, Brumpy, decided to live with us at the same time. Since Delores and Brumpy were both teenagers and sweet on each other, one of them had to go. It was Delores, but Brumpy did not stay long after she went home.

Ernie was religious and had been raised a Methodist but refused to attend church; I had also been raised a Methodist, was no longer religious but thought our children should be taken to church for some fundamental teaching in ethics and morals. I was fortunate that Orange was one of the few communities near us that had a Unitarian Church, doubly fortunate in that we could walk to it. I did not join but embraced it and attended with the kids for several years. Sally Crystal also attended the Sunday school. Fran and I became friends with a number of church members, especially Malcolm and Connie Blodgett and Trygvie and Katherine Bjornson. Trygvie taught both children to play piano; Katherine taught dance classes enjoyed by Fran and me. My reason for not joining was simple. The then current minister believed in emphasizing inner spiritual life; I believed in putting religion into life in the community.

Fran and I on winter Saturday mornings regularly took Sally and Mindy to the ice rink at South Mountain Arena in West Orange where they both learned to skate creditably. Fran fretted, wanting to be skating also, but the ice was restricted to students. I cooled my heels, having given up the sport in college following a bad fall skating backward.

Mindy began going to sleepaway camp early. There were a Scout camp and a nearby private camp for short sessions, both of them disastrous. Then, when she was 10, we found Phyllis Velasquez, of the Gay Head Indians, Wampanoag Tribe, who was running a camp on Martha's Vineyard. Mindy spent two summers there, swimming in the ocean (Mrs. Val said "don't wash off the salt~your skin needs it"), picking the local berries, marveling at the Clay Cliffs in their many colors and the general beauty of the island, and (to the dismay of parents when we learned about it later) helping to empty the cesspool! Mrs. Val's fees were reasonable, but I still developed a habit of designating one of each child's Christmas gifts as a down payment for the coming summer's camp. It was useful; it made for early planning. The second summer, Mrs. Val decided that in addition to girls she could manage six-year-old boys, so Josh travelled up with Mindy on the train. I don't believe we heard a word about boys after that one season.

By this time, our country had already been at war in Vietnam for two years, fighting not only the Vietnamese but their allies from China and the Soviet Union. As it heated up and we learned more about it, we began to attend many rallies and peace marches

7.1 Crystals and Thompsons at Youth for Integrated Schools march in Washington, DC

urging an end. Fran and I, with our children, were constantly leafletting and marching in protests. Frequently these took us to Washington, D.C. There we were lucky to be guests of Julius and Ethel Weisser, outstanding progressives who had headed up the struggle in their city to save the Rosenbergs. One especially clear memory is standing on the great lawn overlooking the White House and singing "Give peace a chance" over and over and over. There was no end in sight.

As a young teenager, Mindy, having done a brave act, came in with a wet, bedraggled, very pregnant cat she had rescued from boys in the park who were trying to drown it. We gave the cat loving care until she produced

7.2 Kittens

six kittens. Mindy named all of them: I remember "Famine" (for the book on Ireland she had just been reading), Spartacus (she'd been reading the book by Howard Fast), and Kareem (for basketball player "Lew" Alcindor who had just taken that name).

In the meantime, by the autumn of 1962, a serious international situation had developed. The US apparently had missile sites around the USSR, which retaliated by placing missiles in Cuba, a socialist country only 90 miles from us. The Soviet Union sent a letter saying it would remove the missiles if the US promised not to invade Cuba. We as progressives went to Washington, D.C. to urge JFK to agree to Khrushchev's proposal and avoid what promised to be the first nuclear war. It was one of the tensest days I remember. JFK did accept the letter and the two sides then established a Hot Line and in August a year later signed a Test Ban Treaty prohibiting the testing of nuclear weapons in the atmosphere.

The summer Mindy was 12, she went to Camp Webatuck, did not enjoy it and ended the season with a badly sprained knee. But by the time she arrived home and had a chance to go to Washington with her father, her spirits revived. Martin Luther King made his famous "I have a dream" speech on August 28, 1963, at the Lincoln Memorial at what King called "the greatest demonstration for freedom in the history of our nation." He said, "We can never be satisfied as long as a Negro in Mississippi cannot vote and a Negro in New York believes he has nothing for which to vote... I have a dream that my four little children will one day live in a nation where they will not be judged by the color of their skin but by the content of their character." It was a thrilling day but three weeks later, a bomb exploded in the basement of a black church in Birmingham, and four little girls attending Sunday school were killed.

The following Christmas, when Mindy was thirteen and Josh seven, is one he remembers as an example of what he thinks Christmas should be: fun and surprising. Mindy wanted false eyelashes so I had bought them for her. Josh and I conspired to wrap them. We found five boxes of ascending sizes, wrapped the gift and put it in the smallest one, wrapped that box and put it in the next size, wrapped that, etc. etc. On Christmas morning, Mindy unwrapped and unwrapped, finally arriving at her gift, to the delight of all.

The civil rights campaign in the United States was heating up. The summer of 1964 was Freedom Summer. The Student Non-Violent Coordinating Committee, called "SNICK," was in full progress in Mississippi signing up unregistered voters. Fewer than 7% of blacks in that state were registered, prevented by high poll taxes, difficult literacy tests, registration made inconvenient and time consuming, and denial of crop loans, not to mention arson, beatings and lynching. That summer became a sad one. In June three COFO[1] workers involved in registering voters, Michael Schwerner and Andrew Goodman, both white, and James Chaney, a young black from Mississippi, were arrested, released from jail, then seized by the Klan, beaten, shot and buried under tons of dirt. Their bodies were not found until August 4. "The Mississippi murders had taken place after the repeated refusal of the national government, under Kennedy or Johnson, or any other President, to defend blacks against violence."[2] A trial was held but the ringleader was not convicted until 2005-41 years later. President Lyndon B. Johnson signed the Civil Rights Act of 1964 but it did not include voting rights.

1   COFO, the Council of Federated Organizations, was created in 1962 by local civil rights activists joining forces with SNCC, NAACP, Southern Christian Leadership Council and Congress of Racial Equality. It organized Freedom Vote in 1963, urging support for Freedom Party candidates, and Freedom Summer, urging support for candidates in the real presidential election of 1964.

2   Zinn, op.cit., p. 456. I recommend reading Zinn's entire Chapter 17, "Or Does It Explode?"

It was important to support Freedom Summer. We organized a group of Mindy's teenage friends to raise funds to send South. In the midst of the campaign, however, she was invited to visit Bermuda as the guest of a niece of our next door neighbors, Richard Saunders, noted black photographer for Life magazine, and his wife Emily. She spent half the summer there and returned speaking the local patois and refusing for several days to speak anything but. Her friends and I were almost relieved when the Blodgetts invited her to Maine for the rest of the summer. In her absence we continued to raise money for Mississippi, to a total of $500, which was creditable for very young teenagers.

Our office at the Center for Constitutional Rights was always part of the freedom struggles going on in Mississippi. Rita Schwerner, for example, the widow of Michael Schwerner and herself a veteran of those struggles, was on the staff. But in addition, before the Center was formed, Bill Kunstler, who was counseled by Arthur Kinoy, had invited Mort to join him in the work he was doing in the South. Mort became more and more involved, on one occasion recruiting almost a hundred other attorneys from New York and New Jersey to participate, at their own expense, in taking depositions on the almost insurmountable obstacles imposed on black voters' ability to register.

It became clear that trying to register blacks in the all-white Mississippi Democratic Party was impossible. The tactic was changed to signing up black voters in the Mississippi Freedom Democratic Party, established in April 1964. A convention was held in the summer and 68 people were picked to run. It included a few white candidates. The delegation attended the Democratic National Convention held in August in Atlantic City but was refused seating. Fannie Lou Hamer, a native of the Mississippi Delta, "the world's worst place to live if you were black," made an appeal to the Credentials Committee that was carried on all the major networks. She reported how she had never known she had a right to vote, that when she tried to register she was forced to leave the place where she had lived and worked for 18 years, and stated that she was "sick and tired of being sick and tired."

Mort remembered that there was a legal move that had been used during Reconstruction to aid a black candidate. Dan Crystal searched until he found it and an action was brought, but the convention still refused to seat the MFDP delegates. It was not until four years later, at the next national Democratic convention in Chicago, that they were accepted.

On March 7, 1965, a small march from Selma, Alabama to Montgomery was called in protest against the inability of blacks in the South to vote. Barely started, the march was broken up with tear gas and billy clubs. Two weeks later, 25,000 people marched. Councilman Ben Jones and Dr. John Alexander attended from Orange. Joan Daly, who met them on the plane by accident, had decided by the end of the day that she and her husband would move to Orange.

It was a happy day for our family in 1965 when we found the Farm & Wilderness Camps run by Ken and Susan Webb in Plymouth, Vermont. They specialized in a Quaker atmosphere, living as close to nature as possible, kybos (toilets) open on one side to the sun and air, swimming in their private lake sans suits, a camp for boys and one for girls in which the campers lived as Native Americans, a night each camper old enough to do so spent alone in the forest, and a garden where teenager campers raised much of the food consumed in the camp, to mention a few of the ideas making F&W unique. It was expensive but, being in need of diversity in the camp, there was some scholarship money available. Josh spent the summer at Timberlake, one of the F&W boys' camps, on a partial scholarship. The next year he went back as a paying camper, the result of our saving all through the winter. Mindy, at 14, got a job baby-sitting for the dance instructor's child at Tamarack Farm, the teen-age camp. She worked mornings and was free in the afternoons to enjoy camp life. The height of the summer for her seems to have been hiking Mt. Lafayette. With all the difficulties she describes in *The House of Joshua* —boots that did not fit, a sleeping bag that was not warm, a backpack that increased the weight to be carried—she nevertheless made it to the top.

Josh enjoyed Timberlake. After that for three years he went to a camp called Darrow, canoeing in Eastern Maine and finally to Canada, earning his paddle. He remembers that paddling 270 miles was routine on a one-week trip, and there were many such trips in the course of a summer. He came home with the biceps to show for it. He loved Maine and those summers were filled with unforgettable memories.

While our kids were going to camp, I began to make efforts to get other children in the neighborhood scholarships so they, too, could enjoy camping. A surprising number of the camps I knew responded favorably, and arrangements were made with several families in Orange to send their youngsters away for an experience of camping. Sometimes it worked out well; sometimes it didn't. Once I arrived back from my yearly visit to my parents to learn that two girls I assumed were happily camping had been dissatisfied and come home.

Josh began to want a dog, and when Josh wanted something, a campaign was sure to follow. He had decided it should be a German Shepherd. I soon found myself, against my better judgment, looking at NY Times ads. I dragged my feet, but he persisted, and we eventually found a breeder in Florham Park, not too far away. We visited, and he chose Ranger. The price was $200. I had only $50 with me, but we were allowed to take the puppy home, and I paid off the rest at $50 a month.

Josh was initially disappointed at Ranger's not having all the attributes of a champion of the breed and thus not being able to become a show dog. But he spent time with him every morning and every evening until Ranger became an extraordinarily responsive and obedient dog. He also took him to a training class. Ranger was doing splendidly in the graduation class

7.3 Ranger with Josh

and on the way to coming in first, when I coughed a little from way up in the stands. Ranger glanced up to find me, was distracted and came in fourth, to Josh's disappointment. At one point, Ranger became terribly thin. We took him to a different breeder who told us we were giving him an inadequate diet. We started making the sacrifice to feed him better, and he responded by becoming strong again.

Josh has a marked talent for making and keeping friends. Among his early friends was a boy who lived around the corner and was considered a little slow. I was sometimes critical, asking him why he didn't play with someone else. Josh was stalwart and unchanging in his friendship for this as other playmates. Some 40 years later, he retains friendships initiated then with Victor Jones, David "Pick" Conley, Edward "Cookie" Green and Gene Lennon.

Through the years, Ernie worked without surcease to build strength in Orange for the emergence of black leadership. The East Ward was organized in CRG. Other wards followed that

7.4 Maggie at Ben's campaign headquarters, photo by Herb Way

example and developed political organizations that Ernie coordinated through Amalgamated Organizations for Good Government in 1965. That same year, he became program director of the Orange Higher Achievement Tutoring Program and served as executive director of the Foundation for Negro Progress. During 1968, he was on the advisory committee of the Title 1 Program in Orange. He also extended his efforts outside of Orange.[3]

3   The "Ernest Thompson Papers" compiled in August 1984 by the Department of Special Collections and Archives, Rutgers University Libraries, states: "Beginning about 1964, Thompson was a labor advisor to the Newark Coordinating Council. The following year he represented the Council on its negotiating committee which lobbied for equal employment opportunities at the Rutgers University Law School and at the Newark College of Engineering construction sites in Newark. As part of this effort, Thompson mobilized the Black elected officials of Essex County.

Ernie cared deeply about gaining opportunities for blacks to work in the building trades. In his book he had quoted the 1963 report of the N.J. Advisory Committee to the United States Commission on Civil Rights,

> ... there are only 14 Negro apprentices out of approximately 3,900 in the State of New Jersey attest(ing) to exclusion of Negroes from the program. The two dominant reasons emerge--lack of information among Negroes about the apprenticeship program and lack of enforcement of the existing non-discrimination clauses.

Paralleling this, and more deadly, was agreement among the craft unions as well as among the building contractors not to hire blacks.

Note should be made of the role of Rebecca Doggett, a charming and brilliant young woman who came under Ernie's tutelage and ever after aided and abetted his efforts while making tremendous strides on her own against jim crow. Even now, almost 40 years after his death and after having retired from her own successful career, Becky continues to work, with ever more success, on a program to gain opportunities for blacks to work in the building trades.

Events in the South having moved at lightning speed, realization dawned that individual efforts were not enough. An organization was needed. Together, Stavis, Kunstler, Kinoy and Benjamin E. Smith, a black lawyer from New Orleans, gave birth in 1966 to the Center for Constitutional Rights.

Although Mindy suffered from bad tonsils, I had consistently refused to have them removed because even bad ones were said to be some protection against bulbar polio, the killing form. Few people now remember how terrible the epidemic was every summer. Two years after Mindy was born, there was the worst outbreak in the nation's history with over 3,000 dead and more than 21,000 left with some form of paralysis. A PBS documentary reported that

---

Meetings with the attorney general and governor of New Jersey led to the desegregation of many of the trades through state enforcement of civil rights laws. During 1968 Thompson founded the Tri-City Citizens Union for Progress and served as the chairman of its organization and membership committee. In 1969 Tri-City, which had operations in Essex, Hudson, and Union Counties, established the "Amity Village" rehab and cooperative housing projects in Newark.

"Apart from the atomic bomb, America's greatest fear was polio." It was not until April, 1955, that Dr. Jonas Salk's vaccine was declared "safe, effective and potent" and it was still later, after development of the Sabin vaccine, that there was a national Sabin Sunday on April 24, 1960, when everyone in the country was urged to take the oral vaccine--no shots. Our whole family lined up that day for the pill. I have no remembrance of why I still made Mindy wait until she was 15 for the operation. The surgeon who performed it said they were the worst tonsils he had ever seen.

Mindy's 15th summer was spent at a National Science program in D.C. She remembers that she and I realized she would be graduating from high school after three years and that for the National Science

7.5 Ernie's 59th birthday party; left to right: John Alexander, Jimmy Murphy, Larry Gordon, Ernie Thompson

program to appear on her record she had to go at 15 rather than the usual age of 16. We were able to work that out and she spent the summer at Howard University.

In the summer of 1966, I suddenly felt so over-worked and tired that I decided not to work any more, so advised Ernie and Mort, and simply stayed home. A day or two later, I received a ticket from Mort for a Caribbean cruise to five islands. It happened that Ernie's 59th birthday was that week and I had arranged a party for him. It was a fabulous affair with great food and drink and everybody in Orange of any significance putting in an appearance. At the end I broke down and cried. I woke the next morning to find I had to leave immediately for the cruise. Someone helped me pack and rushed me to the proper pier.

It was my introduction to the Caribbean. We were unable to land at the Virgin Islands because some U.S. vessel was moored where we would have docked. This was a real disappointment because my Orange neighbors had alerted their friends to expect me, but I relished each of the islands we visited–Puerto Rico, where I spent the day with Meyer and Shane Kushner, who were engaged in the hardware business; Guadaloupe (very lush), Saint Lucia (very poor) and Barbados (an enchanting island). I resumed my home and office duties when I returned but told Mort I could not work so hard and voluntarily took a wage cut. I also told Ernie, but it was harder to lighten my home burdens.

It was about this time that Mindy needed a new bed. Buying a real one was out of the question, so we purchased a solid door, attached six-inch legs and bought a mattress to fit. She slept on it for a number of years, but not alone. In the mornings I would find, snuggled in with her, two of the cats and Ranger, our German Shepherd dog, now full-grown. I thought then it was generous of her. Should I have worried that she was letting her friends take advantage?

In April of 1967, there was a union affair. Ernie and I rarely had a chance to socialize so we went out for the evening, leaving Mindy to take care of her brother. When we returned home we found she had swallowed aspirin, had second thoughts, taken Josh by the hand, walked to Orange Memorial Hospital, about 10 blocks away, and had her stomach pumped. When I learned this, I did the classic, unforgivable thing. I said "How could you do this to me?" I then moved heaven and earth to get help for her, finally finding a black male psychiatrist in Newark. His policy was not to talk to parents, so I never knew, and still don't know, the results of that experience. I know I suffered almost more than I could endure throughout the entire time, frantic being a mild word to describe what I went through.

That summer, Mindy got a job working for the anti-poverty program then in existence in Orange. For an entire summer she planned and carried out two trips a week for teenagers to programs of interest in New Jersey, once including a weekend in Washington, D.C. It was a responsible job and she rose to the occasion. I had promised her a vacation when the summer was nearing an end.

By that time, all her friends had had their ears pierced. The practice was for them to do it for each other at home in the bathroom using a regular needle. I refused to let my daughter take such chances but finally allowed her to have it done by a doctor. She immediately left for Puerto Rico, staying with Catherine Korman, a friend who had been active on the committee to sponsor a Robeson concert. Mindy's ears became badly infected. The medical system in P.R. then consisting of clinics spread around the countryside, she had to bicycle several miles every day to one of those for treatment. She had some delightful time on the beach, however, and got a really bad sunburn.

Mindy's high school career lasted three years. She had two friends whom I got to know and like, Herb Way and Bernadine Oliver. She was given a silver flute and, with help from here and there, learned to play but holds it against me that we could not afford lessons. She was missing one history course needed to enable her to graduate at the end of her junior year. She took that in Newark and was graduated with high honors from Orange High School on June 22, 1967. In the meantime, she had applied to and been accepted by a number of colleges. Bryn Mawr was chosen because it offered a full scholarship, and she entered there the following September.

In July of 1967, a riot broke out in Newark, starting with a minor altercation with a cab driver. It raged from the 12th to the 17th. We could stand on our stoop in Orange and hear the gunfire. It was not the first. Riots had been taking place in a number of U.S. cities starting in 1965. The disturbance in Newark left 26 dead and $10 million in damages. It was criticized as "a shopping spree (by rioters) and a shooting spree (by authorities)." As soon as the shooting stopped—while the tanks were still in the streets—Mort phoned me to meet him at the office. He joined Willard Heckel, Dean of Rutgers Law School, in calling together leading citizens to end the violence and reconcile differences. He also undertook representation of the cab driver in defense of the criminal action against him.

On April 4, 1968, Dr. Martin Luther King, Jr., only 39 years old, was assassinated by James Earl Ray in Memphis, Tennessee, where

King had gone to support a strike of sanitation workers. The whole country was stunned and saddened. Riots broke out in 100 cities. There was a national day of mourning and a funeral attended by 300,000 at which one of King's speeches was read, calling for us to "feed the hungry," "clothe the naked," "be right on the (Vietnam) War question," and "love and serve humanity."

That summer, Mindy travelled to Europe with Ina Gordon to attend the World Youth Festival in Bulgaria. I felt lucky that she was going there instead of Haight-Asbury where a small revolution was going on. There were good movements against the Vietnam War and for black liberation but also many snares for the young. In preparation for her trip, we went to Doop's, a high-end shop on Central Avenue in East Orange, and bought her a stunning, stylish, colorful, washable dress for the trip. The Vietnamese War, which had started in 1964, was still on. She was useful in translating the French spoken by the Vietnamese to the young people assembled from around the world. When it ended, she and Ina enjoyed the luxury of the black sand beaches on the Black Sea before setting off for Italy. There they traveled on bicycles to see the sights. Apparently they found the Italian truck drivers happy to provide rides upon occasion.

In the meantime, Walter Conkite had declared the war unwinnable. College campuses erupted against it. When I called Mindy at college, the phone in her room was answered "Committee to End the War," a sign that she was working hard on campus. The draft was mocked. Three hundred American boys saying "Hell, no, we won't go," emigrated to Canada. Mohammed Ali who had been sentenced for draft evasion asked the government to void his conviction. The Smothers Brothers, Arlo Guthrie, Springstein, and "Alice's Restaurant" all helped to mold public opinion for peace. "Make love, not war" became a popular slogan.

Eugene McCarthy, a Senator from Minnesota and a strong critic of the Vietnam War, ran for president in 1968. We became very much occupied in doing what we could to support his campaign. Ernie ran as a McCarthy delgate in the Democratic primary and Ben Jones began to speak publicly for peace.

McCarthy did so well in the New Hampshire Democratic primary that President Johnson announced he would not run again. Robert Kennedy entered the race when it became clear there was popular sentiment against the war, but tragically he was assassinated. There were bitter struggles at the National Democratic Convention in Chicago that summer, with the anti-war protesters battling literally thousands of troops and national guardsmen. Our office was to become involved and work hard for years defending seven of the leading protesters who were arrested. All were eventually exonerated. The Democratic nomination went to Hubert Humphrey who opposed Richard Nixon and lost.

Josh had become enamored of football, so I sent him to a football camp in the summer of 1969 when he was 13. While there, he was able to watch Neil Armstrong on TV as he became the first man to walk on the moon.

At Bryn Mawr, Mindy played an active role, doing well academically, leading the peace movement and later starting a movement for a Black Studies Program. But there were no boys and almost no black students. Near the end of her freshman year, she applied to the University of Chicago and was accepted. Ernie suggested she consider what she owed to the peace movement. She stayed. Near the end of her sophomore year, she applied to Princeton and was accepted in the first class to include girls. Ernie suggested she consider what she owed to the Black Studies Program. She stayed. I bought her a used VW so she could get off the campus to visit Philadelphia on weekends.

The committee for a Black Studies Program met and negotiated with Dr. Herbert Aptheker, an eminent historian, to become a professor at Bryn Mawr, and for Ernie to conduct a weekend seminar on race relations. Both commitments were kept. The course was established and the seminar was held.

In Mindy's junior year, 1969-70, support for peace kept growing, with a march on Washington in November numbering 500,000. In February 1970 we learned of the massacre at My Lai. On April 30, President Nixon announced his intent to invade Cambodia. Students at Kent State University in Ohio demonstrated in opposition, and the National Guard fired 67 rounds in 13 seconds, killing four, two of them women, and wounding 12, one of whom was permanently paralyzed. There was nationwide protest, with four million students going on strike. Days later, 12 black students at Jackson State University demonstrating for the same reason were attacked, with two killed and nine wounded. (An odd thing is that I can find extensive reports on Kent State and almost none on Jackson State.) President Reagan, speaking on the student unrest, said, "If it takes a bloodbath, let's get it over with."

A popular slogan was "Hey, hey, LBJ, how many kids did you kill today?" Joan Baez and Bob Dylan constantly sang against the war. The show "Hair" contained the words "The draft is white people sending black people to fight yellow people to protect the country they stole from the red people." Publication of the Pentagon Papers by the NY Times on June 13, 1971 clarified the issues. A subsequent article in 1996 stated that the Papers "demonstrated, among other things, that the Johnson Administration had systematically lied, not only to the public but also to Congress, about a subject of transcendent national interest and significance." In January, 1973~six years after Martin Luther King had called for an end to the war~Nixon announced he was ending it,but it was not finally concluded until 1975. It was the longest war in our history, with over 58,000 of our service men and women being killed. Huge numbers of Vietnamese, Cambodians and Laotians also died.

Ernie had been warned in 1963 that the kidney disease which ran in his family and had killed a younger brother was attacking him. The knowledge scared him for a few days, but then he resumed his hard work and life-style. Nobody warned me how serious the situation was. In 1968, I realized he had earned a vacation and scraped up enough money to send him to Barbados, one of the places I had visited on my cruise~a stunningly beautiful island, with a Prime Minister who had married a former resident of Orange and with an average income of $25 a week (as opposed to neighboring Saint Lucia, where the figure was $10 a week). Ernie had been there only a few days when he had a stroke. Because his reputation had traveled with him, he was cared for in the hospital at the expense of the Barbadian government, and when he could travel was sent home accompanied by a young woman doctor. He made a miraculous recovery from that stroke, but had another stroke, and in the years that followed suffered major health problems.

The doctors in CRG had divided up responsibility for our family, a pediatrician taking care of our kids and an internist taking care of Ernie (I had my beloved Dr. Tushnet). The doctors found that Ernie had seven or eight aneurisms and needed an operation urgently. I called his sister Lorraine Jones in Pennsylvania.

The day his father entered the hospital, Josh told me he had heard Johnny B. Lawson play and he wanted to learn guitar and he wanted to start on an electric guitar and he needed it at once. I felt this was his way of alleviating his concern about what would happen to his dad. In addition, when he was eight, he had taken piano lessons for two years and his teacher had told us he had talent. So I spent many hours with him that day shopping for the right guitar. He remembers that we paid $83 for a Sekova electric guitar. He was 14 and already six feet tall. Ernie was on the operating table almost all day but survived. The relatives arrived that evening to the good news.

The history of his being on the kidney machine is interesting. He became very ill and was taken by ambulance to East Orange General Hospital where his case was so mishandled that there was no recourse but to transfer him to Beth Israel Hospital in Newark, where he was put on dialysis for the first time. Thereafter, he required dialysis three times a week. Since he was wheelchair bound, transporting him to Newark was a major problem. He needed a machine at home. There were two obstacles. Machines were scarce. If there were one available, it was not going to go to a black person.

Finally, Ernie's friends were able to convince the authorities that he was a person of such importance to the local community that having a machine in his home was of paramount importance. Pressure was put on me to run it. I adamantly refused. One could bleed the patient to death in three minutes on that machine if one were not apt, and I knew I was not apt. CRG approached Murl Daniels, who was then a student at Upsala College in East Orange on full scholarship, to do the dialysis, paying her for her assistance. She went on to become a teacher in Newark for 25 years, but while still a student, and as long as Ernie lived, she came to our house faithfully three times a week, accompanied by her young son, Seth.

During the summer of 1970, Mindy had helped Ernie write his book, *Homeboy Came to Orange*. A talented and helpful Montclair artist, Don Miller, designed the cover and illustrated key chapters.

The draft of his book completed, Ernie had another heart attack on the evening of January 25th. He died quietly at home, as he had requested. He was 63. His body was cremated. There was a small family service at Woody's and a memorial service at Union Baptist Church on Oakwood Avenue, attended in large numbers by Ernie's friends and admirers. There is no way to better convey the content of the service and the summary of Ernie's life and work than to reprint portions of the tributes paid to him. Dr. Alexander said:

> Dear God, Ernie Thompson just arrived in Heaven a couple of days ago. You may not know he's there yet... He helped direct one city election from a hospital bed and he negotiated a quarter million dollar agreement within one week after discharge from the hospital... When he first came to Orange, he'd been in a tough fight then, too. He fought for principle with a major labor union and he fought the red-hunters in the federal government over employment equality for blacks, women and all minorities.
>
> When he took on a fight he studied the situation thoroughly. He always warned us that Johnny-come-lately ain't supposed to whip the champ but he showed us that superior preparation can overcome superior forces.

And Mindy, in her tribute, quoted Ernie:

> Mankind has no more time for war, for exploitation, for poisoning the earth. We must learn to live together. The problem in the United States of people living together is a black-white problem. The separatists, be they black or white, have come upon the scene too late. They are only in the way of mankind's preparing itself to live

together.

She concluded:

> Though we still need him and he is irreplaceable, he has left us stronger. He has left behind a bridge for us to cross— the bridge of coalition politics, the bridge of program.

Mindy went back to school. For her senior honors thesis she wrote the first history of the National Negro Labor Council and was later awarded $750 as a grant from the American Institute for Marxist Studies (AIMS) for this pioneering work. She graduated from Bryn Mawr cum laude with honors in history and a Woodrow Wilson Fellowship to study history at Yale.

ENTR'ACTE
ERNIE

He was born Ernest LeRoy Thompson, called "Ernie," and dubbed by the leaders of his union "Big Train" because as a skilled negotiator he could deliver benefits and wage increases.

Even as a boy of 10 or 12 living in the South, he knew right from wrong, knew when his people were being treated unequally and was willing to fight for what he knew was right. He left the South at an

E 4.1 Ernie with Josh

early age, moving to New Jersey to live with an aunt. He attended an evening high school so he could earn money as a pin boy in a bowling alley. The work was hard and the hours long, so Ernie organized the other boys to demand better conditions. The boss confronted them, all the others backed down, and Ernie was fired.

After high school he got a job as a sandhog on construction of the Holland Tunnel, a job so dangerous that the men used the slogan, "Think twice, you only live once." The job was carried on under high pressure, requiring a lengthy stay both before and after work, first to become accustomed to the pressure in the tunnel and then after work to become decompressed to avoid the bends. The men worked behind enormous shields to remove mud, blast through rock and bolt together a series of iron rings that would form the lining of the tunnel. There were over 500 cases of the bends, none fatal. Ernie was one such case, requiring him to go to the hospital and miss a day's work. That day his entire crew was killed when a section of the tunnel collapsed.

Ernie went to work at American Radiator in Bayonne. The company's policy was to keep the workers divided: Anglo-Saxons were in mechanical and warehouse jobs, Italians in first test, Poles in core and second test, and blacks and Hispanic workers in the foundry. The factory was hot and dirty, and the employees put in long hours for low pay. Ernie eventually organized them into an independent union and then into the United Electrical, Radio & Machine Workers of America (UE), CIO. After that, he was invited to join the staff of the UE. He became the first black organizer of an international union in this country.

While leading a strike in Jersey City, Ernie learned that Mayor Hague was mobilizing to overwhelm the union's picket line with a massive assault by armed officers and guards, some mounted. To their surprise, when they arrived the next morning in huge numbers, they found one solitary woman walking the picket line. There were some red faces among the Jersey City constabulary.

Early on, Ernie was told that that he could not organize whites and should confine his efforts to black workers. His experience had taught him that black leadership was accepted if there was common ground, and he continued to act on that knowledge.

Among his qualities was his ability to work with people of differing views and his talent for being far-sighted. During WWII, he was elected secretary of the Hudson County CIO Council, the only black leader of an organization representing thousands of white workers.

Years later, when there was a movement among black unionists to organize nationwide, it was not surprising that Ernie was chosen to be the Director of Organization for the new National Negro Labor Council. He was liked and admired, his integrity and dedication could not be questioned, and he had the organizing skills to do the job. And when the NNLC was hounded to death by the government, Ernie was the one with the guts to go to Washington for its funeral, telling the government exactly what an arrogant, unlawful and undemocratic persecution it had committed.

His family, his sons and daughter, his grandchildren, his associates in CRG, and all who knew him across the country in the labor movement mourned his death. As for me, I never attempted to remarry, knowing I would not find his like again and not wanting to settle for an ordinary life.

> He was a gift.
> In a world that has grown cold,
> He was there with his warmth.
>
> In a world that has forgotten what to believe in,
> He was there with his faith in all things good.
> In a world too filled with "me, me, me,"
> He was there with an unselfish heart.
>
> In a world all cluttered with static,
> He was there with his quiet wisdom.
> He was a gift.

VIII
ORANGE AFTER ERNIE
(1971-1985)

I begin this chapter with a statement of some hard-earned wisdom. It is easy to become an alcoholic. It is hard to endure alcoholism. Alcoholism can be overcome if one is given loving help. For some years before Ernie's death and six years after, I lived in various states of alcoholic fog. It had been coming on gradually. I had been raised in a teetotaler family and learned to have an occasional drink with Cliff, but Ernie liked to drink. He found it useful in his work and a joy in his time off. In the 25 years we were together, I gradually joined him. It was hard on the kids. Mindy was in college for three of those years and home for part of the last one, having been summoned to help Ernie finish his book. The heaviest burden fell on Josh, who had to live with me day after day. He tried to keep me sober. I remember him taking a brand new bottle of Scotch and pouring it down a drain, to little avail. As soon as I could find some money, I bought another. The very most difficult times were those days when there was no money.

It was just three weeks after Ernie died, that I had a call from Lu saying that my Dad had also died. It had been a normal day. He took his walk in the desert and was doing his "setting up" exercises in the living room when he had a cerebral hemorrhage. He was gone in the minute it took Mom to reach him from the kitchen. I went to Tucson for the funeral. He was buried in his Mason's apron. He had lived a good life, and many came to honor him. I had the privilege of giving the obituary. Mom was brave, but he had been the center of her life for over 50 years. From then on, she would simply wait to join him. She took him back to Morgan County for burial.

I often had need of a quiet hobby. I found needlepoint and enjoyed it with enthusiasm for many years, completing about 100 pieces--pictures, pillows, eyeglass cases, wall hangings, coasters, door stoppers, a guitar strap~the fly in the ointment being a piece I designed myself and worked on for two years. It was to be a pillow for Josh's piano bench. When I proudly presented it to him, he found it to be too high (the foam rubber insert was then about an inch). It was taken apart and remade to fit an insert

8.1 Needlepoint

of half an inch, but by then he had a new piano bench, half as long as the original. My pride and glory languishes in a closet.

Throughout my marriage, I maintained contact with my family, going to Chippewa Lake, or later Tucson, to visit once a year for a week. It had developed that my Dad was so prejudiced against my marriage that I could not take my family home or expect my parents to visit us. But I could not find it in my heart to break off relations with them completely. Hence the brief yearly visits. I was later to learn that Mindy was unhappy about them, but I could not have lived with myself otherwise.

After Ernie died, 397 Olcott Street became a ghost house. No one came to see us. There were no meetings. Hardly anyone phoned. Then Joan Daly became my friend. Over the years, she and her husband, F. Albert, known as Al,

8.2 The Dalys

became the family I didn't have, incredibly kind and generous. Al owned a moving company started by his father. Joan had worked in high school for Hahne's, an upscale department store in Newark, becoming a buyer. After marrying, she went to college, acquired a Master's degree and when the kids were in their teens, went to work as one of the pioneers in the new Head Start program, then became a contract specialist for the State's Social Services program, and retired

From One to Ninety-one ~ A Life

after 25 years.

The Dalys are deeply religious Christians. When I had cataract operations, it was they who took care of me. When I was abruptly dismissed from rehab, it was they who welcomed me to their home. It was Joan who joined me in coin collecting, doubling the fun and excitement. I was a fixture at their festive annual Christmas, New Year's Eve and St. Patrick's Day parties, and at Easter dinner. Over the years, I enjoyed knowing their sons, David and Doug, and their granddaughter, Leah. It was through them that I met Marjorie Westfall, a dynamic woman who after retiring as a teacher joined the Peace Corps and served in Papua, New Guinea.

In the spring of 1971, Josh dropped out of high school. I was beside myself, but his music teacher told me that he was not paying attention in any classes except his and that Josh might as well stay home and "work on his ax." Mindy was at college. I had no one to consult. I did not seem to have a choice. He taught himself to play guitar.

Josh worked hard on his guitar and soon accumulated other aspiring musicians his age. They assembled at our house daily after school to play rock and roll, and they played it loudly. An Italian family living in the big house to our south took to calling the police and complaining. I had to race home after work to beat the cops and/ or lower the level of sound. In those days no one dreamed of locking his house, or even his cupboards and closets. My Rollei disappeared along with both my wedding rings.

After Ernie died, Mindy finished her honor thesis on the NNLC and was graduated from Bryn Mawr with honors in history. She received a Woodrow Wilson fellowship to Yale University to study black labor history. Mort hosted a luncheon after the ceremony for her family and friends.

It occurred to me that a dog would be a perfect gift for her as a graduation present. I knew she wanted one, having lived her entire life with animals. I bought her a beautiful German shepherd dog named Shana. Just then she started dating Michael Kaufman, a young sports writer. He couldn't tolerate dogs. Shana came home to stay. Two rambunctious large-breed dogs in a small house were too much. Shana had to go, so I donated her to The Seeing Eye in Morristown to be trained as a guide dog for a blind person. Later they expressed regret at being unable to use her because an examination revealed she had hip displasia and could not tolerate strenuous work. Shana came home again.

One morning Josh walked both dogs to the park, neither he nor I realizing that Shana was in heat for the first time. They had barely entered the park when Ranger mounted Shana. Josh was acutely embarrassed and, not knowing what else to do, walked them back across the street still coupled. I called the veterinarian who said we could either be patient or we could try a bucket of cold water, but the important thing was to bring Shana immediately for a shot to prevent pregnancy. We did. Shortly after, I learned that Tommy Edgerton, who had been a good friend to Ernie, was moving to a farm in North Carolina where Shana would have freedom. I gave her to him but to my sorrow learned a few months later that she had been struck by a car and killed. She was a sweet little animal, eager to please, and deserved a better and longer life.

Later that summer, Mindy married Mike. She was 20 and so sorrowful over the death of her father that she rushed into marriage. The wedding was held on Martha's Vineyard where they were vacationing. Josh, a friend of his and I went up a day early. We stayed with Hannah who had a vacation home on the Island. Mike's parents came up. Ben Jones came up. Mort and Esther came up, bringing the wine. Their luggage was delayed, and Mort arrived to give the bride away in the clothes he had worn sailing their boat. The liberal rabbi— willing to marry a Jew and a non-Jew—I had searched for and found, arrived. I had hoped to have a black minister, our friend the Reverend Ulysses Blakeley, as well but could not afford the extra expense.

Mindy and I had shopped and found a white cotton Mexican wedding dress, both becoming and affordable. She wore yellow roses in her hair and looked beautiful. I hosted a dinner that evening at a local hotel. It turned out to be a joyful affair until I spoke, saying how happy Ernie would have been if he could have been there. At that, I put a damper on the occasion by breaking into tears.

I enjoyed getting to know Mike's parents, Jack and Yetta Kaufman. He was a manufacturer of women's dresses in New York City. I found him remarkably relaxed and wondered why. It developed that early on he had realized that every woman needs a black dress--for funerals, religious services and similar occasions. Those dresses do not need to follow the latest fashion in hemlines and styles; as a matter of fact, the more conservative, the better. So Jack was freed from frantically keeping up with the latest trends. He made becoming, sensible black dresses, and women sought them out. It was a brilliant decision on Jack's part!

Following the wedding, Mike and Mindy moved to Connecticut so that she could attend Yale University on her Woodrow Wilson fellowship to study black labor history. There was a train to New York that allowed Mike to commute to his job. But she found Yale totally lacking in the research materials she needed to begin her studies. The next time I heard from her she was selling stockings in Bloomingdale's. They moved back to New York City and bought a co-op in Washington Heights. As she wrote in *House of Joshua*, she got a job in Columbia Presbyterian Hospital as an office worker to help Local 1199 organize the workers.

After working as a secretary at Presbyterian Hospital, Mindy got a Master's Degree in Nutrition, took other courses and applied to study medicine. When she was accepted at Columbia

8.3 Mindy with Dina, Molly and Kenny

University Medical School, she convinced Mike, who wanted a child, to adopt Kenny in 1975 and Dina three years later. They had Molly Rose in 1979 when Mindy was on her internship as a psychiatrist. They divorced in 1982.

Soon after, Mindy met Bob Fullilove. By spring they had decided to marry. He got a job at the University of California at Berkeley and she at the Tenderloin Mental Health Clinic in San Francisco. They rented a house in Berkeley. He put his and Bobby's belongings in a

U-Haul and took them to Englewood, where a garage sale was held, reputedly the best in the neighborhood that day because prices were so low. There was no time to hold anything back, and everything was on its third or fourth time around, anyway. The house, a veritable castle I hated to see go, sold in two weeks. Mindy's car was sold, and Mindy traveled to Berkeley with three children, stopping in Chicago long enough to give a speech. For the time being, Kenny and Bob's son from his first marriage, Bobby, were to be living with Bob and Mindy, Dina and Molly with Mike.

I was inveigled into going to Berkeley to help with the unpacking, which I did, staying two weeks. We had some fun mixed with the work, seeing Fran, who took us all horseback riding, Roy and his wife, who were visiting, and of course Sally, who lived in Oakland near the Berkeley hospital where she was a nurse.

At some point during this decade--I cannot pin down the exact date--Mort invited me to accompany him, his wife and a small party on a trip to China. It promised to be very worthwhile, but there was a rift between China and the Soviet Union and I sided with the Soviets. I knew I would be uncomfortable on such a trip, and I regretfully declined to go. Only once did I get to visit China. Years later I was in Hong Kong and had a chance to go to Canton Province for one day. It was a full and rewarding trip that gave us brief glimpses of both rural and city life. I bought a pearl ring I have to this day and I did not run into any overt politics.

At 15, Josh was reading widely, including books on vegetarianism. He became convinced that not eating meat was the healthiest way to live. I agreed to change but dragged my feet, not wanting to and not knowing how to make the transition. He finally put his foot down. I bought some books and studied them, learning that vegetarian cooking is more complicated since care has to be taken to make sure enough nutritious ingredients are included to make up for the missing protein in meat. From then on, it was a struggle to keep him happy and well fed on a strange new regimen.

By now I was working daily with numerous young lawyers and law students, and I picked up their language. In those days it frequently and constantly included the f-word. Our house was a gathering place

138

for teen-age musicians. Josh called me aside one day and told me that my use of that word was inappropriate. I never used it again.

I do not know when it happened, but I discovered that Mindy's high school friend, Bernadine Oliver, was homeless, her mother having taken a dislike to her politics. I invited her to live with Josh and me. Then I discovered that she was ill. I sent her to a doctor I trusted to be examined, but we got no definite

8.4 Bernadine Oliver

diagnosis. I kept sending her to this doctor and that hospital until there was a decision. She had multiple sclerosis. There was no cure at that time; I don't know if there is one now. She was an outstanding young woman--beautiful, bright and talented. A scholarship was arranged for her to go to Mt. Holyoke, but after some months, she returned to us. She lived with us, even had a love affair, but found life in Orange limited and uninspiring. She moved to New York City among friends. A book of her poetry was published, but she remained an invalid and did not live long.

After Ernie's death, I became interested in coins. Years before I had tried to collect Roosevelt dimes (which still had silver content) but money was so tight I often found myself "borrowing" a dime to help pay the 15 cent bus fare to work. That was temporarily the end of my collecting, but I never forgot what fun it had been. Much later, I began to collect again, this time indiscriminately--Lincoln head cents, Indian head cents, buffalo nickels, Washington quarters, Morgan dollars, even a few gold coins. My enthusiasm infected my friend Joan. We joined the local coin club and in two different summers traveled to seminars in Colorado Springs and Penn State University. My passion continued for many years. I loved modern coins, early coins, ancient coins, US coins, foreign coins, and I collected as often and as many as I could afford, Morgan dollars being my special passion but all of them being cherished. Perhaps the jewel of my collection was a silver half-shekel from the First Revolt. But closest to my heart were the slave tokens with their brave cries for equality and freedom.

In 1972, a CCR case, in which Mort was lead counsel and Doris Peterson co-counsel, involved representing the Gainesville 8, members of Vietnam Veterans Against the War accused of conspiring to disrupt the Republican National Convention in Miami Beach at which Richard Nixon was picked to run for president. What were they accused of using to attack the convention? Slingshots. The case was scheduled for trial in July. Our team travelled to Florida and stayed in a hotel for the duration. The defendants lived in their cars or vans and mostly subsisted on peanut butter sandwiches. It was revealed that the VVAW had been infiltrated by the FBI, and it was agents provocateur who had committed any illegal acts. Scott Camil, a defendant, said, "Our conspiracy ... was to go down to the convention and exercise our Constitutional rights."

Before the trial started, the VVAW and supporters set up a camp in the woods outside of town. Pete Seeger came to sing, and Tom Hayden, one of the principal founders of Students for a Democratic Society, was there. I still have a ring, made from an enemy airplane downed in Vietnam, that Tom was wearing and gave me. We had been friends in Newark where he was a community organizer. Anthony Russo, one of the publishers of the Pentagon Papers, came. And Ron Kovic, author of *Born on the Fourth of July*, a powerful story of life in the Vietnam War, visited. He had been paralyzed from the chest down and had undergone excruciating ordeals in rehab before becoming an anti-war activist.[1] Hundreds of veterans came to demonstrate and leaflet before the trial began .

At the trial, John Kniffin, who had had three helicopters shot down under him, told the jury: "We have asked for an end to war

---

1   Oliver Stone filmed Kovic's book *Born on the Fourth of July*, with Tom Cruise playing the lead. It came out in 1989 and won two Oscars and a 3-1/2 star rating.

and the government has called us traitors. We have asked for justice for all citizens and received billy clubs ... and an indictment." The government's star witness was revealed as an FBI informant. When the jury got the case it reached an decision in four hours. All were exonerated! It was a hard-fought but gratifying victory for the people. Besides the ring, I have another souvenir. The wives of the defendants occupied the long waiting time with needlework. They gifted me with a patchwork quilt pillow showing a standing rifle holding a helmet, the universal symbol of a soldier lost in battle.

Among my most cherished memories of that trial is the following. The morning after the victory celebration, everyone headed for home. Everyone except Mort. During all the weeks we had used the large room in the hotel which was our assembly point for discussions, strategizing, planning, and the other times we all had to be together, some of the furniture had taken a beating. On that last day, Mort arrived with some tools and plenty of glue and proceeded to put the damaged pieces back together, avoiding what could have been a rather large bill to the Center, not to mention a black mark against our name.

That same year, Josh turned 16 and learned to drive. I bought him a used VW. He went back to school, and got his High School Equivalency. After that, he attended Essex County College where he enjoyed his association with Kenny Barron, an outstanding pianist and head of the music department, and Aaron Bell, bass player and composer who had worked with Duke Ellington. The following year, he attended Livingston College, one of the branches of Rutgers University, where he worked hard. In the fall I enrolled him again, but after a week or so he decided not to attend and came home. He was determined to master the guitar on his own. He later told me he could have saved two years if he had been willing to take lessons. I had bought elegant, matching bedspreads for him and his roommate; he came home without them.

Josh was offered a job on the road with Charles Earland's band. They toured for several months, including two appearances in New York at Mykell's, a famous New York nightspot.

Every day, even on the road, Josh worked at weight-lifting and body-building, achieving a 32-inch waist and 44-inch shoulders. He entered at least one contest for weight-lifters, finishing 4th in a field of 25.

In 1975, almost five years after Dad died, Mom broke a hip and after a few months slipped away at what she maintained was 86. My sister became

8.5 Josh (right) bodybuilding

suspicious, did some investigating and learned she was actually eight years older than that, making her 94. She always was a gallant lady, bearing with dignity and courage whatever was her lot. Her body was brought back to Ohio for the funeral, which I attended. She was buried beside Dad in her beloved Morgan County. She left me the astounding sum of $10,000, saved with who knows how much patience and determination. I never learned from her the secret of saving: I immediately split it between my two kids, each needing a car.

Eddie Andrade and Becky Doggett worked with me in presenting the manuscript of Ernie's book to various publishers, without success. The only answer was to do it ourselves. In 1976, Mort gave me two weeks off from work to learn to run

8.6 Homeboy Came To Orange cover

a typesetting machine. Evenings I would visit the Kaufmans in New York and Mike would edit the next chapter or two for me. At the end of two weeks, it was in the printer's hands, with Dr. Alexander and a group of CRG members picking up the tab. Two weeks later we were able to hold in our hands Ernie's dream of "Homeboy Came to Orange" to serve as a guide for the future.

Josh went to Bermuda in 1977. He wrote me, "Having fun in the sun." I have no clue as to why he was there or what else he did. That year he cut his first records under his "Homeboy" label. His group "Sputnik" dominated our lives, having all its rehearsals at the house, not to mention that most of them also "pumped iron" there.

I went to the New Outlook Peace Conference in Israel in 1977, traveling with Ruth Glassman. Going to England, we were jammed into a BOAC plane so filled with smoke it was almost impossible to breathe. Even I, who was then a smoker, suffered. But once we arrived in Israel, the trip became thoroughly rewarding. We were lodged in a beautiful hotel in Tel Aviv overlooking the Mediterranean. It was November and too cold to swim, but the view and the sunshine were breath-taking. And the breakfasts, served buffet style, included the most delicious breads and cheeses and fruits and eggs.

There were delegates from around the world, 400 in all, half Jewish and half Arabic. The air became electric when we learned that Prime Minister Menachim Begin had invited Egyptian President Anwar Sadat, and he was coming to visit. People across the country stayed up all night to produce Israeli flags that flew everywhere, the planes that had been constantly on guard stopped flying and a wonderful quiet enveloped the country. It was a moment to be cherished as Begin and Sadat discussed peace and laid the groundwork for an Israeli-Palestinian agreement.[2] One indication of Israel's need for peace was that it was using all but 5% of its possible fresh water supply. Only regional agreements for desalinization plants would permit more growth.

The balance of that trip was also wonderful. It should be noted that shopping in Israel is not uncomplicated. Moslem establishments

---

2   Sadat and Begin jointly won the Nobel Peace Prize in 1981 but Sadat was isolated and snubbed in the Arab world. In October of that year he was assassinated by Moslem terrorists.

are closed on Friday, Jewish shops on Saturday and Christian ones on Sunday. I visited a shuk in Jerusalem, went to Yad Veshem and reverently placed a stone on the grave of one of the Holocaust victims, went to the West Wall and the Via Dolorosa, and saw much of the Israeli countryside being made green by reforestation. Ruth knew a family who had emigrated from the U.S. We visited them and got an insight into real life in Israel. It was harder than life here and required dedication and courage from the new settlers, but everywhere there was building, building, building.

I saw the golden dome on the great Baha'i temple in Haifa only from the air but, having worked with a Baha'i follower, I was thrilled at the

8.7 Josh and the band that went to Cuba

sight of it. I became friendly with a remarkable Arabian man and his wife from England who attended and supported the Israeli peace conference and its objectives, and I had time in London to sight-see with them. They took me to Ye Olde Curiosity Shop where I bought the two ceramic Dickens heads I still cherish.

1978 was a big year:

-for Josh, who resigned from Earland's band when he learned that he could take his own band to Cuba for another World Youth Festival. His was the only jazz group from the US. He wrote me: "Having the ultimate trip, a super fantabulous time. Manana we play Lenin Amphiteadro in front of (hopefully) 20,000 people." He reminds me that his group included "Cookie" Green, Victor Jones, Stephen Powell and Mike Moseley.

-for Mindy, who was graduated from medical school, richer by $500 as "one of five winners of the Franklin McLean Award for outstanding minority medical students in the U.S."

-for Murl, who found her first house and bought it, moving to Union-and, alas, farther away from me.

The birth of Molly Rose Kaufman in March of 1979 made that a banner year. She was an adorable baby and grew up a sweet and delightful child. She had the blessing of being cared for by Regina Turay, a smart and loving woman from Africa, for many years while her parents worked.

8.8 Molly and Dina with Rosie

Missing a dog, I bought Rosie, a standard poodle, dark grey, almost black. True to her breed, she was affectionate, trainable and, most important, did not shed. She had one weakness: car sickness. Molly, about four, looking dear and dressed for a wedding, received the brunt of one such sudden attack. I was upset and Rosie was sorry. Mindy simply put Molly in the tub and the dress in the washing machine and in due course they went to the wedding unperturbed. In 1981 I enrolled Rosie in the beginners' class of the K-9 Obedience Training Club of Essex Co., held in South Orange, and in June she won 4th prize. She was my dear friend until I moved to Hoboken, when I had to give her away, along with my cats, because the apartment building did not allow pets.

Later that year I finally got help from Mort and Mindy and entered New York Hospital in White Plains for treatment as an alcoholic. I was a good patient, being accustomed to therapy from having once attended an overnight session with Mindy and Mike. After about a week, the office called me in to say they could not find insurance coverage for me. I assured them I had carried it for years. It turned out I had forgotten to make the most recent payment and had to go. I was there for only eight days but I did not panic. I knew it was all right. I did not have a drink for 13 months and since then have faithfully had one a day before dinner and no more. Like Ivory soap, I strive to be 99 and 94/100th% pure on that score.

In February of 1982, Mort and Esther invited me to take a trip with them. The rich and rewarding itinerary, thoughtfully worked out by Esther, included a flight to London and then to Barcelona for four days, then via Rome to Nairobi to Salisbury (Harare), Zimbabwe, where we stayed with Noel Galen and his wife, Doris Peterson, for nine days, enjoying their suburban home, complete with swimming pool. For me there was only one hitch. My luggage went to Rome and did not return until the day before we left. Being without one's "stuff" is off-putting, but I borrowed here and there and bought a swim suit in Harare.

Doris was involved in a massive work: Compiling a system of law that included a) tribal law, b) the British colonial laws and c) the laws that had been developed since independence. Noel was one of only four psychiatrists in the country, so his volunteer work was extremely useful.

While in Zimbabwe we saw many wonderful sights, including historic Great Zimbabwe in the south. This involved a long trip by rented car during which we had to be constantly on the alert to keep Mort on the correct side of the road. We drove through the poorer parts of Zimbabwe's farm land. It was only there that we could see some black ownership of land. And we took a short plane trip to visit magnificent Victoria Falls in neighboring Zambia.

From there we flew to Athens for such delightful days of visiting museums,   shopping in the plaza for gifts to take home, and taking an overnight boat trip to Crete that we forgot to catch our flight to Yugoslavia and had to take a special plane to the walled city of Dobrovnik, from there to Zagreb, then back to London. British Airways was on strike so we flew India Airlines home, a perfectly delightful trip, enjoying the special food, special smell in the air, special costumes worn by the attendants.

Over the years, in addition to camping, Josh had some vacations, one to Puerto Rico, where he was taken to be a native even though he did not speak Spanish, and a cruise to Bermuda with me where he made friends with the young musicians on board from Russia. In 1972, when he was 16, he and his band, including Victor Jones. Ed "Cookie" Green and Wilbert "Buttercup" Johnson, performed at the World Youth Festival in Germany. He continued to work on his ax, and the band, playing mainly R&B, began to get jobs, several times earning $500 for a dance at Rutgers or Seton Hall. He began to compose and built up a repertoire. "Cookie" produced Cook's Tune.

Then Josh discovered jazz, dropped all his commercial activities and began daily teaching himself to play it. It took a long time. Learning to play jazz is difficult because it is a new skill. The jazz style and its element of improvisation require concentrated and intensive work. Josh stayed with it.

It was about this time that the main drummer, Kenny Donnelly, found himself homeless and moved in with Josh and me. He had the trait for sickle cell anemia and from time to time had to fight battles for his health. He stayed for several years, a most welcome addition to the family. When he moved out, he left me his hair dryer and two blue and white plates, one by Noritake and the other Willow Ware by Woods. I still use all three. Kenny was indeed lucky to find a wonderful woman who cares about him and takes good care of him. Together they have raised two delightful daughters. Every five years or so, Kenny sends me an elegant bouquet for Mother's Day.

8.9 Kenny Donnelly and family

Jeryl Johnson from Montclair was Josh's girlfriend for a number of years. I was sad to see them break up, but he later found Stephanie Williams from South Orange–daughter of a beautiful mother and an obstetrician-gynecologist father. She was 20, a student at Rutgers Newark, about to graduate and working afternoons in her father's office. She was lovely, and Josh fell in love.

In the meantime, he and his partner, Gene Lennon, were setting up a studio to produce records. They had a lease, had put in steel doors and a phone, and I donated a large air conditioner and helped them buy a computer that would allow them to have one of the more advanced studios in the east.

Somewhere during this period, I began to collect movies. I had always been a fan, seldom walking out of a movie without having been transported to another world from which I had to descend slowly. And I was a collector from my earliest days. It was a natural combination. The movies then available were VHS and I soon filled one, two, three, four bookcases and a special case I had Al Daly build, to a total of a thousand tapes, mainly high quality movies, many meriting three stars or more. It was a source of great joy then and for years. When VHS was phased out and DVD introduced, I bought a machine which played either and could transform a VHS tape into a DVD disc. I have now given the collection and its bookcases to my grand-daughter Molly and my great grand-daughter Lily. It is housed in Mindy's new home and I hope will be a source of enjoyment and education to the girls.

In 1982, McSurely v. McClellan, a case Mort worked on for more than 15 years, came to trial in the U.S. District Court for the District of Columbia. The staff went to Washington for the duration. I lived with Ethel and Julius Weisser. The Medal for Excellence Citation awarded Mort by Columbia Law School six years later quoted from a New York Times editorial of January 15, 1983 that summarized the case as follows:

> Alan and Margaret McSurely struggled for 15 years to vindicate their right to urge social change, read unpopular literature, keep the Government from prying into their diaries and intimate letters. At long last, a jury in Washington, DC. has delivered a ringing verdict; the late Senator John McClellan of Arkansas conspired with Senate aides and Kentucky law enforcement officials to rob the McSurelys of their liberties. The jury awarded them $1.6 million in damages...

> Their attorney, Morton Stavis, asked the jury the right

question: 'What's the value to you of living in a country as free as ours?' The Washington jury gave a thundering answer.

When we returned from Washington, there was a furious week of finishing work in Hoboken, packing and moving the office to the CCR. My first day on the new job, I bought a paper at Penn Station, headed for the PATH and fell over a heavy bundle of papers. I was crippled for several months, during which Ranger kept vigil over me. I was confined to sleeping on the sofa. One night as I lay down in bed, Ranger came from under the piano where he often rested and with a heavy sigh settled down at the foot of the couch to guard me. It was his last unselfish act. We found him there the next morning.

The broken leg healed, but it was a very hard year. The hours were long, and there was much overtime. The commute was three hours a day, sometimes longer. I had an additional problem. I couldn't stand to have anyone out-produce me, so there I was up against all those youngsters (everyone except the director was young enough to be my grandchild, and the director could have been my daughter). I had long ago been taught:

We should do our work as well,
Both the unseen and the seen,
Make the place where gods may dwell,
Beautiful, entire and clean.

So I had not only to do a vast quantity of work, but it had to be as nearly perfect as I could make it. My life became work, walk the dog, sleep, walk the dog, work. I decided that as soon as I reached 65 in another year, I would retire.

In 1983 Josh gave a fusion jazz concert at Rutgers University in New Brunswick. It was a great success and he considered doing more work on college campuses, but there was still prejudice against "black music."

I turned 65 in December 1984. The next day I retired, applied for Social Security and resigned my job, but continued to work at CCR on a part-time basis. In 1985 I began to do some traveling.

In the spring, I went to Mexico on a cruise with Lu and Jim from Los Angeles to Mazatlan, Puerto Vallarta and Acapulco, flying home just in time to join Mort and Esther on a cruise on a chartered sailboat in the British and American Virgins. There were seven of us plus the captain (quickly demoted by Mort to First Mate) and the cook. The average age was 70, somewhat reduced by my being only 65. A great cruise.

Then I went to Nicaragua, with a U.S. delegation made up of Susan Kinoy, Margaret McSurely, two Boston women and myself. We carried medical supplies for which we had raised money. They included a portable EKG machine apparently worth its weight in gold. The Sandanistas had defeated the dictator Samoza and established a democratic government, but the Reagan administration suspended aid and refused to allow export of the country's one valuable product, coffee. Coffee was sitting on the wharves rotting. We stayed about a week, met a range of people, came to understand some of the serious problems facing Central America, and got to visit the beautiful high country where the coffee grows. Following our visit, Nicaragua was hit by Hurricane Mitch in 1998. Over 9,000 were killed, two million made homeless, and $10 billion in damages suffered. It is now one of the poorest countries in the western hemisphere.

In July I traveled to Canada and Alaska on the Nieuw Amsterdam with an old friend from my Zanesville YW days, Miriam Sherwood. Seattle, her home, is a stunningly beautiful city, the boat trip to Canada on a hovercraft was exciting. Vancouver was new and intriguing, with a wonderful museum of Native American art and tea served the British way. Vancouver Island, "home of the newly wed, the nearly dead and the flower bed," was elegant.

The most unforgettable part of the trip was a visit to the Butchart Gardens in Victoria, British Columbia. Here, five gardens have been constructed in an abandoned quarry, each one an example of what happens when art and nature are combined with utmost love. Perhaps only the Garden of Eden was more beautiful than what we witnessed that day.

The ship, on which we traveled to Alaska, was part of the Holland America line and its crew people from the countries Holland had owned, mostly the East Indies. I enjoyed meeting them. In Alaska we visited Ketchikan and Sitka and saw a glacier that even then was sadly depleted from the warming of the planet. When we returned, we spent some time admiring and hiking magnificent Mt. Rainier.

This was followed by a one-week course sponsored by the American Jewish Congress at MIT. The wonderful week in Boston allowed for a successful day of whale watching.

On September 1th, I went to a sailing camp on Deer Isle, Maine, an Elderhostel trip. I learned little about sailing~it rained the entire week~but I enjoyed the other campers, especially a woman who had kayaked around all of Hawaii and even arrived at Deer Isle in her kayak.

On September 15th, I traveled to a Shakespeare festival in Ashland, Oregon, another Elderhostel program. The acting was great but the weather so cold we had to wrap ourselves in the blankets from our beds to watch the performances, all out of doors. There was a splendid Tai Chi program I enjoyed every day, and we spent one day admiring Crater Lake, part of our national parks system. It is the deepest lake in the Western Hemisphere, known for its dark blue color and clear water. Formed by the collapse of a volcano, it fills a caldera 2000 feet deep. I made friends with the other four women who were smokers. Every night one of us climbed up, turned off the smoke alarm, and we played cards. When the session was over, some of them went with me to Roseburg, Oregon, to visit my niece, Sharon Thrall, who was practicing medicine there.

I went to Bermuda with Joan and two other friends on a ship that also served as our hotel. We had some glorious days enjoying the sun and the sights, and we experienced being on an island where everything that isn't manufactured or grown there has to be imported and where the water comes not from wells but from the sky, is caught in huge cisterns and has to be cherished and used sparingly.

On January 6, 1987, I traveled to Tilbury, the Port of London, and boarded the Soviet ship Azerbaydzhan, a converted ferry boat but sea-worthy, for a three-month cruise around the world, stopping at 30 ports.[3] We were a few hundred passengers, all but half a dozen

3   Rotterdam, Madeira, Martinique, LaGuaira, Curacao, Cartagena, transit Panama Canal,

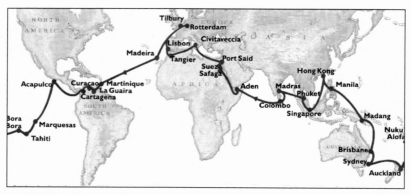

8.10 Cruise route

from England. The trip was a bargain, costing $1,500. I constantly marveled at the wonders I was seeing.

I also made some friends, the best being Bill and Dorothy Olson from London. He was a pilot who had been shot down during the war and suffered lasting injuries. She was an animal lover, a poet and something of a connoisseur. I visited their apartment a year or two later and was amazed at all the beautiful objects, especially the Oriental rugs. And I continue to enjoy a poem she sent me entitled "A Little Litany:"

> For birds with broken wings
> For rabbits caught in springs
> For poor bewildered foxes
> And butterflies in boxes
> For dogs without a home
> For cats that walk alone
> For horses worn and old
> For sheep without a fold. . .
> Lean on us, we beseech thee, O Lord.

I had good health all the way except for a bout of seasickness so bad I swore to the doctor it had to be something lethal.

Our visit to Manila occurred during Corazon Aquino's campaign

Acapulco, Marquesas, Tahiti, Bora Bora, Nuku'Alofa, Auckland, Sydney, Brisbane, Madang, Manila, Hong Kong, Singapore, Phuket, Madras, Colombo, Aden, Safaga, Suez, Port Said, Civitaveccia (the Port of Rome), Tangier, Lisbon, Tilbury.

for the presidency of the Philippines. Yellow was her campaign color; it was a great treat to see it much in evidence. But it was impossible not to see the Manila American Cemetery, beautiful but so vast as to be depressing. It contains over 17,000 graves of our servicemen, most of whom lost their lives in New Guinea and the Philippines, plus the Tablets of the Missing containing an additional 36,000 names of our men lost in Asia.

8.11 Maggie in Tahiti

In Hong Kong I replaced the Rollei that had been stolen with a smaller camera that also had a Zeiss lens, but before I could enjoy it, it too was stolen. To make matters worse, it happened as a result of my attending Sunday services on board the ship.

One of the most thrilling experiences was sailing into Sydney Harbor. The natural beauty of the harbor, plus the size and scope of the bridge and the graceful lines of the Opera House, make seeing it a thrill of a lifetime. But of all the new and marvelous sights I saw, I believe the experiences that most moved me were the hours spent walking among the ancient pyramids, temples and statues in the Egyptian desert and the day spent sailing down the Nile.

ENTR'ACTE
MORTON STAVIS

Sometime ago I wrote a piece that opened: "If Morton Stavis~tireless defender of people's rights, a co-founder of the Center for Constitutional Rights, and my boss~had returned to his office on December 26, 1992, we would have begun our 43rd year together.

E 5.1 Mort

Instead, while on a family trip to California, he suffered a grievous accident on December 18th and died on the 19th."

Here I simply want to note~not his legal career~his record speaks for that~but what kind of person he was, including what kind of boss.

Mort practiced law from the 1930s into the 1990s. Much has been written about his mastery of the law and his use of it throughout his lifetime for the benefit of people rather than as a tool against them. I keep hoping that a definitive biography will be written of this dedicated man. He was brilliant; he was learned in the law and staunchly devoted to the Constitution; he was dedicated to his clients and tireless in pursuit of their objectives; and his sympathies were with the powerless, the homeless, and the disenfranchised.

It should be noted that he finished Columbia Law School with honors before he was 21, and then became one of FDR's " bright young men," assigned to prove the constitutionality of the Social Security Act. He later worked with Senator Wagner to revise the New York State constitution.

He cared about working people and became a union lawyer for the

UE-CIO. He learned about the aspirations and problems of black people and threw in his lot with them. He recognized the need for strong organizations to fight today's battles and, together with three others, founded the Center for Constitutional Rights and served as its president until his death.

At one point, nine women, all of the secretaries who had worked with him over the years, signed the following statement:

> We don't remember your taking a case you thought would hurt the people, or refusing one you thought would help, unless time would not permit. We don't remember your ever turning away a people's case or even a poor person's case for lack of funds; we do remember literally hundreds of matters, large and small, handled without fee. We remember some cases that were lost, but none for want of devotion and diligence. We remember courtesy extended to other attorneys, loyalty to associates, fairness to employees, and support and encouragement of women, minorities and young people in the law. We remember that every day you turned the practice of law into an exciting challenge and commitment to people that dignified your work and ours. Thanks, Mort.

IX
HOBOKEN
(1985-2007)

9.1 Staff of the Center for Constituitional Rights. First row: Julie Cherry, Mort Stavis, Esther Stavis. Second row: David Lerner, Gina Cestero, Margaret Carey, Jane Ransom, Randy Scott-McLaughlin, Maggie, Betty Bailey, Rafi Anglada-Lopez, Marilyn Clement, Yvette Torres-Frankel, Anne Simon, Audrey Seniors. Third row: Sarah Wunsch. People missing from the photo: Claudette Furlonge, Margaret Ratner, Michael Ratner, Joan Washington, Ellen Yaroshevsky, and John Copoulos (who took the photo)

My job had moved to the Center for Constitutional Rights as Mort became increasingly involved in its program. Finally, his children grown and his wife working, he gave up his private practice and concentrated on the work of the CCR. It made too long a commute for me~three hours~so I left Josh living in our house rent-free for a year. During that time he shared it with Stanley Jordan and his family. Stanley was a world class musician with an innovative guitar technique called Two Hand Tap. Both struggling musicians, he and Josh for a time performed on the streets of New York in order to eat.

I moved to a three-room apartment on the fourth floor of 915 Clinton Street, Hoboken, owned by Applied Housing, Joe and Walter

Barry's company. It was across the street from Columbus Park. I lived there from the fall of 1985 to July 13, 2007, 22 years.

Hoboken was for years populated by German, Irish and Italian immigrants. It was full of churches and bars and so poor and run-down that it was a favorite joke of comedians. Applied Housing, with moral and sometimes financial backing from Stavis, came in and renovated 1,500 housing units. This brought in hundreds of new people, and prices rose dramatically, with the result that many of the former residents were displaced. Being just a few minutes from New York City by train or ferry, young career people found it a delightful bedroom community.

I found it an easy commute to work in the city. I joined the Friends of the Library where I made two friends I still see once a year and enjoy- Brigid Cahalan and Yan Li. I signed up with the evening classes held yearly at the high school for a course in movies, but at our first session it became clear there were too few people to make the course feasible. I invited all those who were there to come to my house once a week so we could run our own course. They came. We met for almost two years and enjoyed many fine evenings. My movie collection was invaluable. Hoboken had an excellent adult school, held in the high school across the street from me, where I took a free course in creative writing that I enjoyed.

That year, by a stroke of luck, I had a trip in March and April to Indonesia, sponsored by Columbia University, the Audubon Club, the Chicago Art Institute and the California Historical Society. My boss and his wife had planned to take the trip, but a new case intervened, Mort being retained by the Aquino government to represent the Philippines in its effort to retrieve some of the money stolen by Marcos, particularly New York real estate. The Stavises sold one ticket and gave the other to me. We flew to Hong Kong, staying at one of the finest hotels in the world. I used our one full day there to go to People's China, visiting Canton Province. We then went to Bali where we spent two days seeing lots of dancing, museums, art galleries, wood carvers, and a batik factory. I bought a painting of ships with batik sails that still hangs in my living room and a woodcarving I gave to Stephanie.

We then boarded a small, elegant Greek ship, the Iliria, for the balance of the trip, sailing to Sulawesi and Java. We visited Taraja Land, the home of the boat houses and strange burial customs involving burial in the ground for as many years as it takes the family to accumulate enough for a big celebration, whereupon the deceased person's body (now a skeleton) is disinterred and hoisted many feet to a deck built on the side

9.2 Taraja

of a rocky cliff. We saw several empty decks, the skeletons having been stolen. In Java we visited Borobudur,[1] world's largest Buddha temple, built in the 9th century and one of the greatest monuments in the world. It was lost for centuries, covered up by the jungle following an earthquake and volcanic action.

Ten days later we landed in Singapore. It must be seen to be believed. It's so beautiful, a land of trees and flowers. Their public garden was all orchids! And squeaky clean. A ticket just for dropping a cigarette butt on the ground...

Then back to San Francisco and a visit with Mindy and Bob in Berkeley. As I recall, I helped them make plans to remodel their house before I returned home.

In June of 1987, I finished a course in tutor-training and thereafter worked with a big, gentle 48-year-old moving man with a genuinely nice wife and five children. He was a product of Brooklyn schools and could not say "thing," it was always "ting," but he had a lively mind and an adequate vocabulary (that he couldn't yet read or spell). His goal was to pass the exam to get a driver's license. He achieved that, much to his personal satisfaction and improved income. My next student was a city official in one of the municipalities of Hudson County. He was accustomed to getting by with the assistance of his

1   "The structure, composed of 55,000 square meters of lava-rock, is erected on a hill in the form of a stepped-pyramid of rectangular stories, three circular terraces and a central stupa forming the summit... the whole in the form of a lotus, the sacred flower of Buddha."

wife. His motivation to do his own reading was poor and so was his progress.

I noted in the spring of 1989 that the dollar was down in value, that "our unemployment figures are so gerrymandered it's impossible to know the truth but the number of homeless is rising alarmingly... in the 5th Ave.-53rd St. subway-six blocks from Tiffany's, Bergdorf-Goodman and the Plaza-dozens of homeless men are living."

The 50th anniversary of my graduation from high school occurred and I went to Ohio to attend. Of the 19 who were graduated, six of the men had died; everybody (including me) was overweight; most were retired; several of the women were widowed. But what most disturbed me was that not one of them had changed his/her ideas in 50 years.

My 70th birthday arrived in December. I was afraid my friends would give me a party (and just as afraid they wouldn't) so I went to spend the holidays with my sister and her husband in Tucson. It was the first Christmas Lu and I had been together for about 45 years and brought back many childhood memories, mostly happy ones. In the desert we found the skeleton of a cactus tree, hauled it home and decorated it for our holiday tree, not an original idea but a real western touch to the celebration.

On February 1, 1990, Mindy and Bob, having lived through California's earthquake, moved east to join the faculty at Columbia University. They rented a house three blocks from me and began house-hunting but found prices sky-high. A 4-story brick town house such as I had bought in 1948 in Jersey City for $5,000 was now in the range of $225,000 and, if it had been modernized, could go for $400,000. They eventually bought a house and lived in it for several years. They enjoyed Hoboken but not the house, which they called "the thin house." They sold it a few years later and moved to Englewood, N.J., to an old and spacious dwelling with lots of land. It was convenient to their work, just across the Hudson River via the George Washington Bridge. They lived there until 2010, when they sold it.

I travelled to Europe in September that year, to Paris, Basel, Florence, Vienna, the Black Forest, etc. then added a visit to Ireland.

Our time in Paris was entirely too short; Basel was dark and uninspiring; I was shocked and saddened to see how devastated the Black Forest had become; Vienna was enjoyable for its coffee shops and faded elegance; and Ireland was spectacularly green, scenic and friendly.

9.3 Swiss clock shop, where Maggie bought her clock

I think it was in 1988 that Molly, then 9, and I took the train to Montreal, met Mindy and Bob, and visited both that city and Quebec. I know it was from the 10th to the 17th of June. I suspect Bob's infatuation with things French began there. I remember my first French meal. I wondered where the food was--the plate was barely half-full. The tunnels leading from store to store, so necessary during the long, cold winters, fascinated us. I lost a favorite watch and in general do not remember the trip with pleasure, having been as always somewhat in awe of Bob and not comfortable in his presence.

In May, 1989, I took a 10-day trip with Murl through the South. We visited her Aunt Ossie in Alabama and went on to New Orleans for a few days, thoroughly enjoying the food, the jazz and the culture. I remember buying a magnificent pair of antique gold earrings that I gave to Mindy and riding on a street car where we met the pianist of the jazz band we had seen the night before. We then traveled to see Murl's son, Seth, who was in the Army at Ft. Benning, Georgia. He proudly showed us around, including how he could make a bed so that a quarter would bounce off. He had little free time for us because his girl friend had also come down from New Jersey. We then visited my grandson, Kenny Kaufman, a student at Morehouse College in Atlanta. Morehouse is a men's college with an impressive array of graduates, including Dr. Martin Luther King, Spike Lee, Samuel L. Jackson and many, many more. Kenny was glad to see us; his room was a total disaster; he took us to visit the companion girls' school, Spellman. After that, he, too, had limited time for us.

In 1990 I took a two-week Saga trip in Great Britain and Scotland. A wonderful guide, Don Hylands, traveled with us and won all our hearts. We started in London, stopped in Plymouth to see where our ancestors came from, then went up the west coast of England, seeing Wales, Liverpool, the Lake District, where I enjoyed visiting the home of Wordsworth and seeing the field where, after the early death of their daughter, he and his wife planted the 10,000 daffodils he had immortalized in poetry. We stopped at Loch Ness but failed to see its famous Monster, went on to Glasgow where we did see the royal Scottish jewels, pale in comparison to the British, and had the dubious privilege of eating haggis, a kind of sausage made of sheep heart and liver, cooked in a casing. York was fun because of the architecture and Stratford-on-Avon exciting because of our knowing something about the bard. When the trip ended back in London, I was able to spend a couple of days with my friends, Dorothy and Bill Olson, from our round-the-world cruise.

One day in December, 1992, I received an unexpected call from Mindy, asking if I would meet her and Bob; they wanted to talk to me. I did, only to learn they had been alerted to tell me that Mort had died. He had been visiting his brother-in-law while on a family vacation in California and, while descending from an outside deck, had fallen headfirst into a large tree, been taken to a hospital and put on life-support, but because of the seriousness of his injuries, the plug had been pulled the next day. He was being brought home for burial. My life, as I had known it for 42 years, stopped. There was a funeral; there was a larger memorial service. Mort had lived a great life. He was greatly honored, greatly mourned and greatly missed.

My connection with the CCR ended abruptly. The only person who kept in touch with me, encouraging me to come to some of its affairs, was Franklin Siegel. I shall always remember him kindly for his extraordinary sensitivity then and even up to the present.

9.4 Franklin Siegel

In 1995 a routine mammography revealed a breast cancer. On the x-ray it was ugly–totally, totally round, unlike the outlines of any other part of the breast. I was given radiation but was told I was "too old" for chemotherapy. A lumpectomy was done at Hoboken Hospital, and I recovered without delay or distress. In fact, the surgeon did such a good job–I wished I had had money to have him reconstruct the other breast!

In 1999 I took a cruise on the QE 2 with Stephanie's mother, Claire Williams, Claire's cousin Joyce Easley, a retired teacher, and Edith McClure, then 90, known as "Brittie," another of Stephanie's relatives.

9.5 QEII – Maggie, Brittie, Claire, and Joyce

We visited Cartegena, Colombia, at our farthest point but in the meantime enjoyed the luxury of traveling on that beautiful ship, mystifying some of the passengers who never could figure out who we all were, and just being together with leisure time to enjoy each other.

The 21st century began auspiciously but, as the world knows, at 8:45 on the morning of September 11, 2001, an airliner crashed into one of the 110-story twin towers of the World Trade Center in New York City. Minutes later Joan called me and I turned on my TV to see the second plane crash into the second tower. Nearly 3,000 people died and 6,000 were injured. Another plane crashed into the Pentagon and a fourth into a field in Pennsylvania after crew and passengers intervened. The US invaded Afghanistan to depose the Taliban, which had aided and abetted the al Qaeda terrorists. Nine years later we are still there, still at war, and there is no significant peace movement against it.

In May of 2001, Dan Crystal died. He was a loving man and had lived a dedicated life. At his memorial service I said the following:

> We here are privileged to have known Dan. He was a member of what some are calling 'the greatest generation.' And today, along with his life, we celebrate the lives of two others who in swift and stunning succession have also left us for greener pastures, Dorothy Leavy and Frieda Gordon. All three worked in Mort Stavis's office at one or another time and brought the highest work ethic to their jobs. All three respected and loved each other. Dorothy's husband Tom was Dan's best friend from college days.
>
> All shared a deep love of democracy and a hatred of racism and fascism. They loved learning and beauty and culture. They loved their country and their families. They loved food and music and fun and friends. All felt the slings and arrows of Senator Joe McCarthy, especially Dorothy whose husband Tom lost his job following a HUAC hearing in Newark. They were principled and incorruptible.
>
> They gave of their time, money and strength for what they believed in: the building of a better society. Each of them was 'the purest kind of a guy.'

In April of 2002, Mindy received a second honorary degree, this one a Doctorate of Humane Letters from Bank Street College of Education.

A month later, Molly's family and friends treked to Amherst to see her graduated from Hampshire College. That weekend, it snowed! In May! But it failed to put a damper on the occasion. Mindy played a major role as the graduation speaker chosen by the class.

Another month later, I went to the Cambia Center for the Gifted Child in Brooklyn to see my great-granddaughter Lily (then still using

9.6 Lily graduating

her birth name of A'Lelia) "graduate" from kindergarten with academic recognition in math and a merit certificate for leadership qualities. What a season for reaping pleasure from three of the smart women in my family!

During the summer of 2002, Fran asked me to put on the computer the cook book she was working on. She came to visit and we spent about a month working on it. She took it home, illustrated it with her own drawings, found a relative to print and bind it, and *The Hale and Hearty Cook Book* by Frances Hale was born. She published it in November. It is a charming collection of recipes--all guaranteed to be reliable and delicious--collected over the years from Fran's friends and family.

THE HALE AND HEARTY COOK BOOK

Pear Tree Farm
Leicester, N.C.

Frances Hale
November, 2002

9.7 Fran's cookbook

In January, 2004 I wrote my kids, Ernie's kids from his first marriage, Ben Jones, Murl Daniels, the Dalys, and Becky and Joe Thomasberger that, while it had been our hope that Ernie's ashes could be taken to his much loved Eastern Shore of Maryland, circumstances never permitted it. Homeboy having come to Orange, it was finally concluded that Orange was an appropriate resting place. We came together at the Rosedale Cemetery on the 31st and solemnly placed the ashes in Niche 4467. Then, as I am sure Ernie would have wished, we had a breakfast in his honor.

On March 20th of that year, President George W. Bush led us into another war, this one against Iraq on the theory that it had atomic weapons, in spite of repeated assurances from various agencies of the UN that it did not, and on the never proven suspicion that President Saddam Hussein was harboring al Qaeda. Efforts were made to say the invasion was multinational, but that was largely unjustified. Iraq was occupied, and President Saddam Hussein eventually executed. By the time I left Hoboken in 2007, 35% of Iraq's children were orphans. No significant peace movement ever developed here in opposition to this senseless and fruitless war.

I have an ego wall--a very small one--on which will be found the honors bestowed on me, including: a Certificate of Life Membership in the NAACP, 1988, (painfully achieved over many months in which the organization allowed me to contribute $50 a month until I got to the required $500); a Certificate of Appreciation, instigated by Mindy and signed by family and friends in 2002, at a time when my life was at a low ebb; a certificate of my induction into The Clara Barton Sisterhood of the Unitarian Universalist Church in 2008; a certificate from HANDS as part of its 2008 Leadership Awards for "Helping unite communities for social change"; and an honorary Doctor of Freedom degree from the University of Orange, June 2009. I am especially pleased to be associated even remotely with Clara Barton, a rebel who said:

> I have an almost complete disregard of precedent, and a faith in the possibility of something better. It irritates me to be told how things have always been done. I defy the tyranny of precedent. I go for anything new that might improve the past.

The American Red Cross was born from her revolutionary spirit.

I looked for a Unitarian Church in Hoboken; there was none. I might have settled for a Quaker Meeting; there was none. There are large Catholic churches and less imposing Protestant ones. I had no religious institution in my life for about 15 years. Then I began taking the train to Orange to services at the Unitarian Church, attending fairly regularly. I realized it was filling a real need in my life and I finally signed the membership book. I was also traveling frequently to visit the Dalys in East Orange and Josh and his family in West Orange. It gradually dawned on me that I should move back to the Oranges. Within a month I had done so, settling in South Orange in 2007.

ENTR'ACTE
THE SECOND GENERATION

ERNEST "BRUMPY" THOMPSON

"Brumpy," Ernie's older son, was about five or six when we met for the first time. Ernie was on duty that day as the babysitter and he took Brumpy, his sister and me, with whom he had a date, to a jim crow watering hole for swimming. I don't believe anyone had a good time.

We saw each other from time to time in passing but really met again about ten years later. Brumpy's cousin, Delores, had

E 6.1 Brumpy

come to live with us for the summer so Brumpy decided to move in, too. Unfortunately he and Delores were teenagers and he was crazy about her so one of them had to go. Delores left but Brumpy did not stay long after that.

A few years later, Josh and Brumpy, who bear a striking resemblance to one another, became friends. Josh was intrigued by Brumpy's life, an extraordinary life spent making his living at the racetrack. Brumpy is divorced from a lovely woman with whom he had two bright and beautiful children, Geanine and Michael. She and I exchanged greetings at Christmas time for many years. In recent years Geanine and Mindy have become friends.

MINDY THOMPSON FULLILOVE

Mindy has just celebrated her 60th birthday. She has more than fulfilled all the promise her early life gave. She is strong, loving, steady, imaginative, insightful, and visionary.

After medical school, she

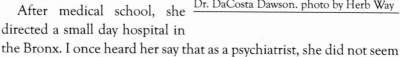

E 6.2 Mindy Fullilove signing her book for Dr. DaCosta Dawson. photo by Herb Way

directed a small day hospital in the Bronx. I once heard her say that as a psychiatrist, she did not seem to have the respect of the staff until one day when someone had a heart attack on the premises, and she saved him. After that, she was respected as a doctor.

Mindy is a board certified psychiatrist. After her move to California, she became staff psychiatrist at the Tenderloin Clinic in the South Bronx of San Francisco and associate clinical professor of psychiatry at the University of California at San Francisco, where she was involved in early work in AIDS, featured in Jacob Levenson's *The Secret Epidemic: The Story of AIDS in Black America*. Back in New Jersey, she is a research psychiatrist at New York State Psychiatric Institute and a full professor of Psychiatry and Public Health at Columbia University. In the aftermath of 9/11, she co-founded NYC RECOVERS, an alliance of organizations concerned with the social and emotional recovery of New York City.

She raised four children to healthy adulthood and now has custody of and is raising a grandchild, A'Lelia Johnson (who likes to be called Lily). Having had parents who loved gardening, she is a natural garden devotee, studying at the New York Botanical Garden when time permits.

Mindy has received many awards for her work, including being named a "National Associate" by the National Academy of Science in 2003, being among the "Best Doctors in New York" and receiving two honorary doctorates (Chatham College, 1999 and Bank Street College of Education, 2002). Perhaps her most treasured honor was being selected to give the commencement address by the 2002 graduating class of Hampshire College, which included her youngest child Molly. I have a note that in 2004, Mindy was one of 14 finalists for Teacher of the Year at Columbia University, with a faculty of over 8,000 teachers.

She writes like an angel. To date, her output includes numerous articles, book chapters and monographs. She is the author of The House of Joshua: Meditations on Family and Place[1] and Root Shock: How Tearing Up City Neighborhoods Hurts America And What We Can Do About It.[2]

JOSHUA PAUL THOMPSON

Josh at 55 is tall, strong, handsome, charming, and fashionably bald. He is also gifted, dedicated, a loving husband, a great father, and a good son. He, too, has more than fulfilled the promise of his birth.

Starting with his acquisition of a guitar at 14, he has been dedicated to music. He dropped out of school at that age, taught himself to play his chosen instrument, gathered a band around him and started performing. He took a group to Germany to play. He attended Livingston College, a branch of Rutgers University, for two years where he studied music. He got a job with renowned jazz organist Charles Earland and went on tour for one year. He then took a group to Cuba to perform. He played a well-received fusion concert on the main campus of Rutgers. In partnership with Gene Lennon, he started a recording company that grew and had some success, the high point being writing for and co-producing Aretha Franklin.

He started his own company, Tallest Tree Music, with a studio in the basement of his home in West Orange, briefly moved to a more elegant studio in Montclair and then returned to an enlarged and

---

1   University of Nebraska Press, 1999.
2   Ballantine Books, 2004.

improved studio in his home.

His work includes: 33 platinum albums, including Alicia Keys, *Songs In A Minor Key* (2002, multiple Grammy nominations and awards); Luther Vandross (2002 Grammy nomination); Joe, *My Name is Joe* (2001 Grammy nomination, Best R&B Album, etc.).

He has also had 10 gold singles and 3 ASCAP awards. Besides the artists named, he has worked with Usher, Babyface, Case, George Benson, O-Town, Tyrese, Alicia Keys and Chaka Khan.

E 6.3 Steph and Josh

In addition to producing, he teaches guitar and is producing his own guitar record with original material, but the projects closest to his heart are producing his son Avery's first demo recording and encouraging Jaden, who now plays the flute.

He pays daily attention to his health and that of his family. He walks, plays basketball, goes to the gym, watches his weight, remains a steadfast vegetarian and encourages his children to do likewise. Recently he has dabbled in cooking, specializing in brunch.

STEPHANIE WILLIAMS THOMPSON

Stephanie's email address, stephaniewhw@etc., says a lot about her. The "hwh" stands for "health, wealth and happiness," three goals for herself and her family she strives for daily.

Stephanie has a B.A. from Rutgers, class of 1985, and has worked in the airline industry for Scandanavian Airlines. She performs accounting and business administration tasks for Josh's business, Tallest Tree Music, L.L.C.

She gets immense enjoyment from rearing her two beautiful

children, Avery and Jaden, the light of her life, devoting most of her time to their health, academic progress, access to the arts and theater, family gatherings, great vacations, community involvement and anything else that may have a positive influence in their lives.

Stephanie is talented and innovative at decorating their home, tireless at keeping the lawn beautiful in all seasons, a housekeeper to put others to shame, a good shopper and an inspired cook. She is also good looking, keeps herself trim and knows just how to dress.

She tells me that she loves "movies, decorating, traveling, live music shows, hangin' with the kids, and laughin' out loud." At big family dinners, I have seen her charm the assembly with her ability to tell funny stories and tell them well.

She had a close and loving relationship with her mother, Claire Williams, who died in 2005. Stephanie remembers her as "the warmest, most non-judgmental person in the world" and still mourns that Claire is not here to share the joy of watching her grandkids, to whom she was devoted, grow up.

With the kids daily growing up, she has begun to plan what to do with the rest of her life, leaning toward her interests in real estate and decorating.

IX
SOUTH ORANGE
(2007 TO 2011)

After living in Hoboken for 22 years, I began to feel the need to move. I was riding the train to attend my Unitarian Universalist Church in Orange, I was riding the train to visit my son and his family in West Orange, and I was riding the train to see the Dalys, in East Orange. Why not move to the Oranges? But where? I began to inquire among my friends for suitable housing.

It was while visiting the Dalys that I inadvertently found a note from Liga Stam on their coffee table, asking them to pass on to me information about the Jewish Federation's Village Apartments in South Orange. I was immediately interested and made a date with Al to take me there. We visited 110 Vose Avenue on a Monday where I met the director, saw three vacant apartments, including an efficiency I immediately knew could not contain me and all my things, liked one with a southern exposure and filed an application. I knew Jeanne Ginsberg, a long-time resident, and sent word to her to please be my reference. I was notified three days later that I was accepted.

I hired Al to pack up my apartment, and on Friday, July 13th, I moved. Because of the impending Sabbath, the move had to be finished by 4:30. It looked as if we would not make it, so I called Josh in West Orange, and he miraculously appeared with three helpers. We got the job done before the deadline. On Monday, Al came back and began putting my house in order.

South Orange prides itself on being a Village, not attempting to provide all that a city could, but making for a pleasant not-too-hurried life. When our family lived in Orange, we knew that our neighbor to the south was a white, middle-class community, the residents being business and professional people, a good percentage of them Jewish. I remember going there twice: to a jeweler where I bought Mindy a brooch showing two white bars (the equal sign) on a black surface, symbolizing racial equality, and to a shoemaker where Fran and I each bought a pair of made-to-order sandals costing the exorbitant sum of $36, and worth every penny.

The Village now has a larger percentage of black residents, necessitating an anti-discrimination committee. The Shop Rite is gone, replaced by Eden Gourmet, selling every conceivable delicacy at upscale prices. Its second floor houses "Above," an attractive restaurant. There are numerous other restaurants. There is a post office featuring a mural painted by FDR's WPA, there is an historic Village Hall, a railroad station connecting the town directly to New York as well as local destinations, police and fire stations, and a public park, a block from 110, with a swimming pool, a tremendous lawn with a hill for sledding in winter, tennis courts, a basketball court, and a building with a small theatre, an art gallery, and programs for seniors. There are a few churches, but many of those, along with the graveyards, were left in Orange when East, West and South Orange pulled away, leaving the center full of tax-exempt properties.

There are two drug stores, three women's clothing stores, a UPS where you can take your camera to be fixed, ice cream parlors, an outstanding kosher bake shop known as "Cate & Abby," a kosher deli, gas stations and a repair shop, a Dunkin' Donuts, a toy store, a Blockbuster, several banks, a cleaner, a locksmith, a florist, a shoemaker, specialty shops, a paper and cigar store, a wine and liquor store, hair-dressers, and a ladies-only gym. But do not expect to go out at midnight for anything!

The Village Apartments, 63 in all, are occupied in the main by single women. State law requires a no-discrimination policy, so there are a handful of us who are not Jewish. The house is clean and well kept, with Monel Delva managing to meet all our needs. The grounds are neat and attractive. During the off hours, we are guarded by either William Raymond Smith (always called Ray) and James Cuciniello (always Jim, of course), who, besides keeping us safe, become friends of all the tenants. When we lock ourselves out of our apartments, as we often do, they do not embarrass us when they let us back in. Our dining room was recently redecorated and is a pleasant place for

FROM ONE TO NINETY-ONE – A LIFE

dinner, served in two shifts three nights a week. Our chef, Angela Heyerdeck, and her staff run a tight ship and feed us nutritiously and well. There is a lounge where we can gather for conversation. It is also used in the afternoons for the knitting club and bridge and canasta sessions. One section of the building provides housing for people needing assisted care.

I live in Apartment 230 in three rooms on the second floor, far and away the best of the three residential floors because it is only one flight up and has access to the parking lot behind the building, thus saving time. I have trees outside my bedroom window so that for several months of the year I do not have to worry about drawing the blinds. There are ample closets, and the trash room is just across the hall, ten feet away. I have resigned from cooking, but there is a well-organized kitchen.

I love my apartment. It is light and airy. It holds all my "treasures"—paintings and photographs, my papers, a few precious books, my collection of American Indian art and artifacts including rugs, vases and baskets, and other much-loved items such as statues and masks from my travels around the world, not to mention my recently acquired "garden." Up until recently, it also held my collection of a thousand movies, now given to a granddaughter and a great-granddaughter.

We have a director named Cheryl Kasye, a young woman who is over-worked, efficient, even-tempered, even-handed and tries to make our lives as full and enjoyable as possible. She has a rare talent, being able to fix almost any mechanical or electronic device one might have.

Two weeks before I arrived, Mollie Weill, retired, and Natalie Hamilton, in her mid-60's and still working, moved in and were assigned to table 2 in the dining room, as was I. We immediately became and have remained friends and still share the same table as well as our ups and downs. Besides them, the two persons with whom I had the most in common were Bernard Kransdorf and Hilda Lipkin. Bernie began to require more assistance than was available here and was transferred by his family to Daughters of Israel in West Orange; Hilda, a former librarian, is as sweet as ever but has begun increasingly to withdraw from our activities, being content to read. I am bereft.

We have an activities director and a program of sit-and-listen activities. I disapprove of it, feeling that seniors need to be physically and mentally challenged and active. I had proposed that she organize a folk-dance evening, but there were obstacles and it didn't happen.

Mollie heads a worthwhile endeavor, the Linus Club, named for the character in the Peanuts comic strip. Volunteers knit 12"x12" squares that are then made into small blankets for hospitalized children. This latter function is performed by Nora Skeados, a Greek lady who has been here since the building opened and who has extraordinary skill and artistry in putting the blankets together. Linus is a national organization and its work spreads far and wide.

Once a week there is a current events program. Almost every evening those who want to talk assemble in the lounge for an hour or two. It's an opportunity to get to know each other and become something like a family. There are bus trips to places of interest in New Jersey and for shopping. There is a religious service on Friday afternoons. There is a purely social Tenants' Association that provides an indoor barbecue in the summer and a holiday affair in the winter as well as monthly meetings. There is the inevitable Bingo every Thursday night. There is Game Night on Saturdays, where Scrabble and Rummycue are played, and there is penny ante poker in the form of Seven Card Stud. It is a semi-closed circle, but if someone else wants to join we have a protocol providing for two tables. I once tried to get chess games going with Bernie Kransdorf as the teacher but only one student showed up.

From the beginning, I have enjoyed the movie program, with showings every Sunday and Tuesday evening. It was run by a genuine movie lover, Irving Schneider, until he died. Since then, I have worked on the program. There is now a committee consisting of Joe Posner, Florence Dove, and Robert Gurwich working with me. Tastes do not run high. Preferences are for any kind of musical at all, but we are interspersing these with the best movies available. My computer comes in handy. I make up the twice weekly notices, attempting to vary format and colors. There are an amazing variety of typefaces available on my iMac and lovely colored papers fairly cheap at Best Buy and Staples.

As soon as I moved here, I gravitated to playing bridge. I had been married to two good bridge players, neither of whom had taught me to play, Cliff because we had almost no time together. Ernie and I played with a couple in Jersey City several times, but I had no idea what I was doing and was absolutely paralyzed with fear when I had to play a hand. I do not know why he never taught me. He had given bridge lessons for a small fee while he was on strike in order to afford his daily diet of a bag of peanuts and a bottle of milk.

Leonard Goldstein, a player of over 30 years experience, and his wife Evelyn, play with us, and Leonard from time to time conducts lectures or Q&A sessions. His presentations are absolutely clear, correct and beautifully done. Whenever this happens, I type up the notes, copy them, and pass them around. It is pure joy to learn how to evaluate a hand, how to bid, how to play the hand and, most important, how to use the conventions~the tools that enable partners to convey essential information to each other in a lawful fashion.

I organized a bridge class that was taught by Theresa Roche. She and I had been friends in Hoboken, both of us moving to the Oranges at the same time, she to the deluxe building at 377 South Harrison in East Orange. I worked hard at encouraging everyone at 110 with the least interest in bridge to Come Down and Play! There is bridge three days a week, and on good days may boast two tables.

In 2008 an event occurred that could not have been more exhilarating and exciting to all lovers of democracy, including one who for 80 years has watched the aspirations of the black people come to fruition. Barack Obama was elected the 44th President of the United States. My heart leaped in joy. I dearly wished I could have joined the cheering thousands in Washington. I follow the ups and downs of his administration, continue to believe in him and hope to see him in a second term. Michelle Obama is also greatly to be admired and emulated.

By the end of that year, the UN reported there were almost five million refugees in Iraq. In 2009, President Obama ordered withdrawal of all but two combat brigades and 50,000 of our troops whose job it is to train Iraqi armed forces. To date, we have lost 5,000 soldiers plus 32,000 seriously wounded. And the cost in money to US taxpayers has been $900 billion, most of it borrowed from China and hanging over us as part of our national debt.

Obama also inherited the war in Afghanistan started in 2001 when the U.S., in response to 9/11, launched Operation Enduring Freedom with support from the British Armed Forces and some Afghan support, with the stated objective of finding Osama bin Laden, defeating al-Qaeda, removing the Taliban, and creating a democratic society.

As of two months ago, there were 97,000 U.S. troops and almost 49,000 from other countries there. Obama has promised to start pulling out our troops by July, 2011. Afghanistan is big, the issues are complicated, the progress is minimal and the cost we are paying both in lives and money is too great. I think we should get out.

I also think that from now on we should follow the advice of General Robert M. Gates, our Defense Secretary, who told a West Point audience recently:

> In my opinion, any future defense secretary who advises
> the president to again send a big American land army into
> Asia or into the Middle East or Africa should 'have his
> head examined,' as General MacArthur so delicately put it.

At the end of summer in 2009, I inherited from Stephanie two plants that had been on her terrace. They thrived. I bought some more plants from Metropolitan Plant Exchange in West Orange, was given cuttings to root and now have almost too many to count. I find the blooming plants a treat, especially in the winter, including African Violets, Amaryllises, Cyclamens, and Christmas or Gyco cacti. I look forward to seeing the Kalanchoes when they come into bloom in the spring. But I also love those that don't bloom but make my apartment a bower, including Corn Plant, Croton, Jade, Aloe Vera, Marginata, Snake Plant, Spider Plant, Bromeliads and Bird of Paradise, plus three or four whose names I don't know but enjoy for their foliage. They all require work but repay in pleasure.

Life has not been all bagels and lox. In April of 2010 there was a catastrophic explosion in the Deepwater Horizon well being operated by British Petroleum in the Gulf of Mexico, 40 miles off the coast of Louisiana. The leak was first reported as 5,000 barrels of oil a day, then raised to five times that amount, or 25,000 barrels (210,000 gallons) a day, resulting in serious threats to marine life and coastal wetlands, vastly impairing the ability of fishermen to earn a living and temporarily destroying the tourist industry.

The 2010 holidays were barely over and we were only 12 days into the new year when an earthquake of a magnitude of 7 hit the island of Haiti, estimated to kill as many as 200,000 people and leave a million and a half homeless. The site was 16 miles from Port-au-Prince, the capital. The machinery of government was destroyed, making it almost impossible for rescue efforts. Tens of thousands had to be buried in mass graves, and an outbreak of cholera, caused by faulty sewer systems, increased the death toll. There is no end in sight to the misery of the country.

A word on the health of the people I live with. There are some with serious vision problems, including glaucoma and retinal deterioration. One woman has had her second Baerveldt glaucoma implant, both successful. Many folks have hearing problems. There are lots of knee replacements, no hips as far as I know. There are a lot of chronic conditions, necessitating numerous doctor visits and some, such as stenosis, requiring valiant daily efforts to exercise. There are frequent falls. There are emergency calls requiring the ambulance. There is sometimes a sadder call for a hearse when there has been a sudden heart attack. There is much to-ing and fro-ing with St. Barnabas, the nearest hospital, often followed by a stay in one of the many rehab centers in the area. Having health problems can become prohibitively expensive, requiring the employment of one or more aides, often to the point the resident has to give up and move to Daughters of Israel. In fact, the great drawback to living here is that one develops more friendships than you would think, and they can and do end suddenly in either death or such disability as to force a friend to move out suddenly to a facility that provides care.

Another source of concern and sorrow to me is that daily I witness the growing devastation in our building. New people coming in may be quite rational but within six months or a year can become shadows of their former selves. Loss of memory and the creeping effect of Alzheimer's disease are taking a terrible toll. I have posted Dr. Charles

Steiner's motto from Plato: "Motion is the source of what is called being and becoming, and inactivity of not being and destruction." I have talked with the director. She has attended sessions run by the Federation people, involving our building and the other residences they run, to instruct the staff in handling those who already have the disability, but they have not established a prevention program, if such is possible, given the present lack of scientific knowledge of the disease.

My own experience is that I found I was starting to lose my memory. I could walk into a room in my apartment and not remember why I was there. I went to my primary care physician, Dr. Debra Goldson-Prophete, who gave me a test. I have always tested extremely well. This time I scored 37 out of a possible 100--shockingly low. She prescribed Aricept, 5 mg, and I started to take it. A few months later, I went back and asked to be tested again. This time I made a substantially better score but still far from satisfactory, so she increased the dosage to 10 mg. I understand the medication cannot recoup what I have lost, but I believe it is postponing further loss for the time being. I tell the people here about it but do not know of any converts. There is new research going on which may prove the pill I am taking is exactly opposite to what is needed. My advice is that it's better to postpone getting any disease, including this one, until all the research is in and the cure found.

I am curious to know if others have experienced the same phenomenon as I. In my younger years, I was an avid reader. I progressed from *Peter Rabbit* to *Alice* to *Tom Sawyer* to *Tarzan*, through a succession of detectives to James Bond and then relaxed with Georgette Heyer. There followed a fairly long period when I did not read but watched movies--at least a thousand of them, including most of the 3-star and 4-star films available. Now I find I have no interest in reading anything that is not of historical or philosophical significance. It reminds me of Edward Everett Hale's story about Phillip Nolan, "The Man Without a Country," who had a similar experience. Is this typical of getting old?

I have now completed four years here. They have been very rewarding. I was able to renew my friendship with Ben Jones before he died. Ben was the victorious candidate run by my husband, Ernie Thompson, and the Citizens for Representative Government to become the first black official in Orange. He served honorably in the city government for 20 years as a councilman, leading the fight for the new high school, revitalizing the city recreation program and ensuring fair hiring practices and equal employment opportunities by the city. Although he was 89 in 2008, he re-organized CRG, this time renamed Citizens for Responsible Government, and served as its president in an attempt to get more democratic program into the upcoming council election. I was elected

10.1 Maggie and Ben

treasurer. CRG met most Saturday mornings in Ben's house. Some dynamic new people became active, among them Pat Morissey, leader of HANDS, and Karen Wells, a retired Wall Street operator who is the unofficial historian of Orange. I found it rewarding to be part of the struggle to find ways to improve the city. Ben and I often went for lunch after the meetings, and it was good to have that time with him. He was committed to his mantra, "I always wanted to help the little people have a better life. Whatever I could do, I tried to do," until his death on June 26, 2009.

It is difficult to overestimate how wonderful it is to have Molly as close as Jersey City, where she lives by night and Orange, where she works by day. Living only a few minutes from Josh and Stephanie and their family has also been rewarding. Josh takes me to doctor appointments too far away to walk; Stephanie takes me shopping; Josh has become an inventive and enthusiastic cook, and I am always pleased to be invited for Sunday brunch. Jaden loves games, is a tough, enthusiastic opponent, and I get a kick out of playing with her. I never fail to marvel at what Avery will come up with next in innovative movie, theatre or musical endeavors. He is also now playing basketball with his school team and doing well. His coach has remarked that he never saw a new player improve so rapidly.

I am sometimes called on to "babysit;" sitting for Avery and Jaden is easy, but Lily is tougher. I attempted to introduce her to some Oscar-winning movies, but she objected and told Mindy I was attempting to make her "cultivated." Recently, however, she has had a change of heart. She asked me to leave her my movie collection, and since I am building a DVD collection, I had my 1,000 VHS movies, and their bookcases, packed up and delivered to her. It is understood she will share ownership of them with Molly.

Commuting by train to the Unitarian Universalist Church was necessarily limiting. Being 15 minutes away by car means I can attend every Sunday, especially since many members live in South Orange and are willing to give me a lift. I cherish the chance to be better acquainted with the other members and to participate more fully. We have been blessed with a succession of three outstanding ministers, The Reverends Tony Johnson, Charles Yielbonzie Johnson and

Darrell Berger, the last being the one I have had the most opportunity to know and from whose extraordinary wisdom I regularly benefit. Our church is unusual in that it is the only U.U. in New Jersey with an urban, as opposed to a suburban,

10.2 U of O graduation

program. This affords us a rare opportunity to try to be helpful in our home city.

Our small church has some extraordinary parishioners, one of whom we lost to death not too long ago. Her name was Jessie Turk. For 30 years she was a college professor. Her subjects were geology and geography and she was as down to earth as her subjects. Most importantly, she had an unfailing sense of what was true, ethical, politically wise and right. And she never failed to stand up from her seat and put us on the right track. I called her "the conscience of our congregation." We still need and miss her.

The University of Orange is a free university of the people, dedicated to learning how Orange can become a Just and Beautiful City. It was founded by and is led by my daughter Mindy and it carries on a program involving participation in civic life, including voting and attendance at one or more meetings of the government, socializing with neighbors, volunteering in some community activity, and taking some of the U of O classes. Among its programs are efforts to help the central businesses and to make Orange "Green and Glowing" by planting trees and lighting the bridges and tunnels. Once a year there is a graduation--to which one must wear a hat in honor of Orange's having been the "Hat City," leading producer of hats in the U.S.--

and those who have completed the requirements are recognized as graduates and a few honorary degrees are awarded. I am happy to be a graduate. Had it not been for the U of O, I might not have been encouraged to volunteer in the program I mention next.

A most important reward has been the opportunity to teach English in a program at our church to Haitians, some of whom have arrived in this country since the January earthquake. I work with women, mostly in their 20's or 30's. They are warm and friendly, eager to learn, have a sense of humor and struggle hard with this not-so-easy-to-learn-language. My favorite, oft-repeated instruction is: "Talk English everywhere, especially at home, and learn from your children!" It generally falls on deaf ears. I was forced to stop when I fell ill but intend to go back as soon as I can. By speaking up, I have been able to increase the tutoring staff. Al Daly is now a volunteer. I shall keep trying. There are many who need help.

Finally, now that Mindy and Lily are established in their new home in West Orange, the most rewarding thing of all has occurred. The whole family will be within shouting distance, as I have become convinced all families were meant to be.

I intended to close this memoir on that peaceful note, but there seems to be "no rest for the weary," all hell having broken out both at home and abroad. At home there is a concerted drive, led by the Republicans and the Tea Party since victories in the 2010 elections, to cut the living standards of the people while protecting those of the 2% who control the majority of the wealth; to slash Social Security, into which we workers have paid our whole working lives, and cut Medicare, which makes possible decent health care retired workers could not otherwise afford. They are even going so far as to attempt to take away a right fought for and won almost a hundred years ago—the right of workers to bargain collectively.

Abroad, it started with Tunisia, spread to Egypt and then to Bahrain, Libya, Iraq, Yemen, Jordan, and, in fact, involving the whole Middle East. Everywhere protesters are demanding change to provide more democracy and a larger share of the national income, and in most places these legitimate demands are being met with violence and bloodshed.

One can only hope that the forces of democracy are strong enough to beat back the excessively conservative in our country and strong enough to win out over the 18th Century-type oppression prevailing in much of the Middle East.

On March 11th, the Sendai earthquake and tsunami struck Japan, doing devastating damage. With a magnitude of 9, it is reported to be the largest earthquake ever to hit Japan and one of the five largest in the world since modern record-keeping began. The tsunami traveled at the speed of an airplane, as much as 500 miles an hour, and produced waves over 30 feet in height. It reached California and Oregon in this country but touched them only lightly.

It is too soon to know the full extent of the loss in human life and property in Japan, but they will be substantial. It is very sad. The complications resulting from damage to the nuclear power plants greatly increase the tragedy. The planet is many billions of years old and its destruction does not seem imminent, but the scientists warn that areas around the Pacific Ocean, including our west coast, both northern and southern, are most likely those at greatest risk for future calamities of the same nature as those that have just struck Japan. We have at least one nuclear reactor in that area.

There has always been one great advantage in living so close to Newark: it has Branch Brook Park, the home of a collection of cherry trees more numerous and more diverse than the famous gardens in Washington, D.C. It is now Spring again, and on a sunny and mild Thursday, one of the few seasonal days we enjoyed, I visited the Park with the Dalys–to admire, to enjoy, to relish, to marvel, and to exult.

I can no longer remember why I thought writing my memoirs was a good idea. It has resulted in many sleepless nights, and much writing that had to be set right by those who lived through the events and then re-written by me. If it strikes you that you may some day do the same, take care to start keeping a diary at the earliest possible date and continue it to the end.

ENTRE-ACTE
THE THIRD AND FOURTH
GENERATIONS

MY GRANDCHILDREN

KENNETH THOMPSON KAUFMAN

E7.1 Kenny and India

Kenny joined the family when he was four, being adopted by Mindy and her first husband, Mike Kaufman. The adjustment from a suburban house with a pool to a small New York City apartment (without a pool) was major, but he took it in stride. Kenny's sunny temper and mischievous smile won him friends everywhere he went. He demonstrated a remarkable ability to manage people and solve problems. His attention to his two sisters did much to create calm in an often frenetic household. He also demonstrated his great athletic ability and unquenchable love of sports. He was on the court or the field from early in the morning until late at night, working hard to perfect his skills, and all the while having lots of fun.

Ken went to Saint Mary's College High School in the Bay Area and then to Morehouse College in Atlanta. After college, he decided to remain in the South, feeling there was greater opportunity for him there than in New Jersey. He married India Phillips, and they settled in the Atlanta area where she became a school teacher. He used his talent at management to develop a consulting business for a messenger company, a daily test of his patience, fortitude and foresight. Happily, he likes to drive and loves to sing, so he prospers in spite of difficulties.

He and India have two daughters, Christina and Hope, who are Kenny's pride and joy. He takes nearly as much pleasure in watching them play sports as he does in playing himself.

DINA THOMPSON KAUFMAN

Dina is a lovely woman with luxurious long black hair, a friendly face and a lively, appealing personality. She is of medium height and build and has a developed sense of style, with good health and a high level of energy. She is a graduate of Hoboken High School and has a certificate in massage therapy.

She has three beautiful children and likes to be a stay-at-home mother

E 7.2 Dina

whenever possible. She loves watching them grow into great people.

Dina recalls my taking her to see "Annie" on Broadway at an early age. It was the beginning of her fondness for theatre and music.

MOLLY ROSE KAUFMAN

Molly Kaufman, third child of Mindy and Mike, is an arresting personality~tall, slender, beautiful and vivacious. She is also friendly, bright, ingenious and industrious.

She went to the Hudson School, a private school in Hoboken founded in 1978 by Suellen Newman. The school's slogan is "Courage, Compassion, Commitment." Molly then attended high school at St. Ann's in Brooklyn (riding the train from Hoboken, often arriving late and always blaming it on the railroad). She graduated from

Hampshire College in Amherst, Mass., on a snowy day in May, 2002, and has a Master's degree from Columbia University in journalism, finishing just when many newspapers were going on line and not hiring. She landed on her feet and is now a community organizer in Orange for HANDS (Housing & Neighborhood Development Services), a very positive influence in the community.

Molly reminds me that she was born under the sign of Pisces. I looked that up.

E 7.3 Molly

It claims she is imaginative and sensitive, compassionate and kind, selfless and unworldly, intuitive and sympathetic but, on the dark side, idealistic and easily led. I agree she has all the positive characteristics; I see nothing wrong with being idealistic, and I do not believe Molly is easily led. So much for astrology.

Molly has, however, found humor in her birthday, pointing out that it is March 14, also known as 3/14. From there it is possible to translate it into 3.14, or the famous pi.

She has had one pi[e] birthday party, starting with shepherd's pie and proceeding through apple, pecan, pumpkin, sweet potato, etc., etc. It was a great success. I recommend that she do this every year with one exception: in order to freshen the palette, every fifth year will be pizza pie.

It is family history that Molly at four rose early, installed herself in the breakfast nook and stayed for hours, visiting with each member of the family as he or she appeared. She still loves spending time with all the members of what she calls her "crazy" family.

Molly likes reading, writing, movies, cooking, playing cards, holidays, throwing parties, family gatherings, travel and the ocean. She lives in what she calls a "cool section" of Jersey City with a roommate and her two cats, Della and Cleo.

ROBERT SMITH FULLILOVE

E 7.4 Bobby and wife, Haruko.

Mindy's second husband had a son from his first marriage, Robert Smith Fullilove, who grew up with Kenny, Dina and Molly. Bobby was identified as a genius early in his school career and skipped a grade in grammar school. In addition to his exceptional academic abilities, he was a talented basketball player who worked hard to maximize his skills. Besides playing basketball, Bobby loves to collect shoes, laugh, write poetry, keep journals and eat large quantities of food. In his youth he had a love for Velveeta cheese that defies description, keeping a large box under his bed in case he needed a snack... or five.

I first met Bobby when he was in his middle teens and his father and Mindy were about to marry. It was Christmas time and both Mindy and I were broke but Bob had a paycheck. We were able to get a modest present for every member of the family. Bobby and I got along nicely and later became pen pals, Bobby sending me some of his poems. I kept them all. Here is a moving sample:

> I and a friend looking for a friend
> Flashing as we approach
> Silliness?
> Or ignorance once again?
> A few run away, a few run towards
> Something happened, something wrong
> Prone body on concrete
> Blood sweeping down concrete,
> Away from anotha brotha
> Rivers to the curb
> Friends holla into the nite air

Young sistas scream out not in joy
For once, cops not assholes to situation
Red and white finally arrive
Uniforms do what they can
Folks just watch.
And pray.
And hope for life.
Medicalized. Stretchered. Placed and taken away.
Future appears over. Life appears obsolete.
At the stroke of midnite to be exact.

His name was Larry. (7/19/96:3a.m.)

Of all his talents and loves, it is his love for basketball that has been the driving force in his life. He has stayed involved in semi-pro and club ball since leaving school. As part of his pursuit of a life in basketball, he went to Japan to play and do other kinds of basketball-related work. He fell in love with Japan. Sometime later, he fell in love with Haruko Takasaki. They were married in Los Angeles and then spent a long year working through the immigration system. Bobby finally got the longed-for visa in the summer of 2010 and left the US to start his new family life in Japan, fortunately not in the region of the earthquake.

AVERY ERNEST ELLINGTON THOMPSON

Josh and Stephanie live in West Orange. Their son, Avery Ernest Ellington, is a delight to all who know him. He is now an 8th grader and has been playing basketball for the first time. He is doing well. His coach says he has improved more

E 7.5 Avery

in a year's time than any student he was worked with in his long career. His team finished the year unbeaten. He has also done well academically, bringing up his grades from mostly B's to mostly A's.

Avery started making his own movies when he was 12, putting them on the Internet. He has now broadened his interests to include singing with jazz bands, saying "Music is very important to me. I'm very good at rapping and OK at singing." He also does impersonations and a Stand Up Comedy Act. Aside from this, he seems to be an ordinary kid, reluctant to do his chores. He says: "Women are important to me because I love girls." He is tall for his age, handsome, well built, strong, affectionate and has an engaging personality. He became 14 in January, 2011.

JADEN SINCLAIRE THOMPSON

E 7.6 Jaden

Josh and Stephanie's Jaden made a biographer's life a picnic by providing me with her profile. She described herself as "shy, sensitive, funny and nice, lover of dogs, reading and games, who feels happy, silly and safe, finds happiness in animals, art and bowling, gives happiness, help and cards, fears Chucky,[1] bugs, and storms while on an airplane, would like to see Costa Rica and Brazil, enjoys vacations, painting and being active, likes to wear Black Dog shirts and a nautical dress..." She enjoys Martha's Vineyard and Jamaica. She recently wrote she would like to be a veterinarian or a writer. (As to the latter, she added: "My teacher says I excel at that."). She was 10 in January, 2011. She is tall for her age, strong, beautiful, with a loving disposition, a winning personality, a willingness to be helpful and a strong competitive sense. While in the third grade, she was reading at the 7-1/2 grade level and

---

1   The scary movie called "Chucky." But she was also afraid of the mouse at Chucky Cheese.

her report card held nothing but A's. This past summer she attended a week-long National Young Scholars' Program in Washington, D.C. for academically gifted students. In the 4th grade she will participate in West Orange's High Aptitude Program (HAP) to learn higher level thinking skills.

In the meantime, she is deeply involved in a campaign to convince her parents the family is incomplete without a dog.

MY GREAT GRANDCHILDREN

A'LELIA (LILY) JOHNSON

Dina's children whom I know are A'Lelia, known as Lily, and Javier. Lily has until recently lived in New York or Bergen County, N.J., so I have not had the pleasure of watching her grow up.

E 7.7 Lily

Lily Johnson was 15 in January, 2011. She is tall and strong for her age. Her parents are Dina Kaufman and Eric Johnson. At age 10 she moved in with her grandmother, Mindy Fullilove, who has custody of her. She graduated from the 8th grade at the Hudson School in Hoboken on June 13, 2010 and is now in high school there. She is a top-notch student, especially in English and other languages, enjoying the study of Latin and looking forward to being fluent in Spanish. She reads two books a day, a passion for reading that began when she first met Harry Potter.

Lily has studied piano and guitar. Her singing is a great comfort to her and her fans. She especially enjoyed singing "The Man Who Can't Be Moved" every evening to her bunkmates at Farm & Wilderness Camp. She is the third generation of the Thompson family to go there. In her third and final summer at Indian Brook, she completed a Pioneer apprenticeship and received a personalized ax. Lily is a favorite of friends and family because of her generous spirit and acerbic wit. She has an infectious laugh and a smile that lights up a room.

CHRISTINA MONET KAUFMAN

"Chrissy," who has always lived in Georgia, "wants to be somebody and make a difference." She tells me she is of average weight and height, in the 8th grade, and jubilant about almost every aspect of her life. It rejoices her to see her entire family together drama-free; it lifts weights from her chest. She is afraid of losing the ones she loves.

E 7.8 Chrissy

Her life revolves around music. She has a deep passion for singing and is teaching herself to play the piano and guitar. She has recently retired from playing soccer but, in addition to singing and playing instruments, loves to act, write, draw and be on the step team.

What does she fear? Spiders, snakes, and lightning. Her list of places she would like to visit amounts to a trip around the world. Bon voyage, Chrissy!

HOPE RAYNELE KAUFMAN

Hope is in the 4th grade and reports that school is going great. She won first place in the Science Fair with the question, "Does the size of a pumpkin affect how many seeds it has?" (She didn't tell us the answer.)

She has long curly hair, is "kind of tall" and

E 7.9 Hope

is a very happy person. What makes her happy? her family, her TV, her room, her house and her friends. Hope also likes soccer, reading, playing with her dog and cooking. She has started her own book about a girl which she hopes to complete when she is older.

Eating is a happy time for her, especially if there is shrimp. She is afraid of spiders and heights. She hopes some day to visit Washington, D.C., New York and Paris, and is torn between being an entertainer and a psychiatrist when she grows up.

JAVIER SMITH

Javier is seven. He is tall and strong and extremely handsome. I am told he likes baseball, riding his bike and playing Nintendo Wii. He is affectionate and sociable and loves his friends.

E 7.10 Javier eating burger

POSTSCRIPT

I was only a child in the lower grades when I learned that there are white people who don't like to see other white people be friends with black people. Thus, almost before I could read, I was thrown into what Dr. W.E.B. Du Bois called the problem of the 20th Century: the color problem.

This lesson was brought home to me again when I was in college. That time I was old enough to begin to understand

Maggie at 91.

it, believe it was wrong, and wish I could do something about it. When I finished college, I went South to learn.

At the end of my life, I am grateful that early on I came face to face with the big issue of my time, one that still faces our country and the world even now in the 21st century. Not to be part of that struggle is to miss life's greatest challenge. Seek it out and do your best.

Langston Hughes, in a few words, brilliantly summarized my credo:

> Not me alone...
> But all the whole oppressed...
> Must put their hands with mine
> To shake the pillars of those temples
> Wherein ...the rule of greed's upheld...
> That must be ended.[1]

---

1   Langston Hughes, "Union," in Arnold Rampersad, editor, and David Roessel, associate editor, The Collected Poems of Langston Hughes, Vintage Books, 1994, p. 138.